THE
EAST-WEST BOOK
OF RICE COOKERY

BY MARIAN TRACY

Illustrated by Marguerite Burgess

DOVER PUBLICATIONS, INC.

NEW YORK

For Caroline Savage

who likes any meal

just so there is rice

Published in Canada by General Publishing Company, Ltd., 30 Lesmill Road, Don Mills, Toronto, Ontario.
Published in the United Kingdom by Constable and Company, Ltd., 10 Orange Street, London WC2H 7EG.

This Dover edition, first published in 1976, is an unabridged and unaltered republication of the work originally published in 1952 by the Viking Press. A new preface by the author has been especially prepared for this edition.

International Standard Book Number: 0-486-23413-4
Library of Congress Catalog Card Number: 76-11517

Manufactured in the United States of America
Dover Publications, Inc.
180 Varick Street
New York, N.Y. 10014

PREFACE TO THE DOVER EDITION

More than twenty years ago, when I wrote this book, rice was little appreciated in this country and seldom came to the mind of those who planned, cooked and ate the meals. Except, of course, for generations of Southerners who have naturally, normally and enthusiastically eaten rice for breakfast, lunch and dinner.

I had been among the ignorant and neglectful ones until I married Nino, whose youth had been spent in the Hawaiian Islands where the family cook was Chinese. From Ah Wong, Nino first began to learn the lifetime joy of cooking and to think rice a habitual and intrinsic part of a meal.

When I began my delighted research into the many, many fascinating and varied ways in which this demure but inspired little grain can be cooked I did not realize how far ahead of the culinary thinking of that time I was. This is not a revised book but a new edition for a revised world, gastronomically speaking.

There is a great change in the availability of types of rice aside from our own good, white rice. I am happy that I can now find the short, stubby Italian variety called *aborio* or sometimes *avorio,* packaged in cloth sacks of one pound. It is much superior for risottos or other dishes in which the rice is cooked in fat before adding the liquid. Rice is one of the first and best of all convenience foods, a blessing for those who are often pressed for time. Except as a crutch for the timid or nervous there seems little reason for instant rice, but all kinds of rice are interchangeable in recipes without disaster—so use what is comfortable for you.

MARIAN TRACY

New York
July, 1976

CONVERSION TABLES FOR FOREIGN EQUIVALENTS

DRY INGREDIENTS

Ounces	Grams	Grams	Ounces	Pounds	Kilograms	Kilograms	Pounds
1 =	28.35	1 =	0.035	1 =	0.454	1 =	2.205
2	56.70	2	0.07	2	0.91	2	4.41
3	85.05	3	0.11	3	1.36	3	6.61
4	113.40	4	0.14	4	1.81	4	8.82
5	141.75	5	0.18	5	2.27	5	11.02
6	170.10	6	0.21	6	2.72	6	13.23
7	198.45	7	0.25	7	3.18	7	15.43
8	226.80	8	0.28	8	3.63	8	17.64
9	255.15	9	0.32	9	4.08	9	19.84
10	283.50	10	0.35	10	4.54	10	22.05
11	311.85	11	0.39	11	4.99	11	24.26
12	340.20	12	0.42	12	5.44	12	26.46
13	368.55	13	0.46	13	5.90	13	28.67
14	396.90	14	0.49	14	6.35	14	30.87
15	425.25	15	0.53	15	6.81	15	33.08
16	453.60	16	0.57				

LIQUID INGREDIENTS

Liquid Ounces	Milliliters	Milliliters	Liquid Ounces	Quarts	Liters	Liters	Quarts
1 =	29.573	1 =	0.034	1 =	0.946	1 =	1.057
2	59.15	2	0.07	2	1.89	2	2.11
3	88.72	3	0.10	3	2.84	3	3.17
4	118.30	4	0.14	4	3.79	4	4.23
5	147.87	5	0.17	5	4.73	5	5.28
6	177.44	6	0.20	6	5.68	6	6.34
7	207.02	7	0.24	7	6.62	7	7.40
8	236.59	8	0.27	8	7.57	8	8.45
9	266.16	9	0.30	9	8.52	9	9.51
10	295.73	10	0.33	10	9.47	10	10.57

Gallons (American)	Liters	Liters	Gallons (American)
1 =	3.785	1 =	0.264
2	7.57	2	0.53
3	11.36	3	0.79
4	15.14	4	1.06
5	18.93	5	1.32
6	22.71	6	1.59
7	26.50	7	1.85
8	30.28	8	2.11
9	34.07	9	2.38
10	37.86	10	2.74

CONTENTS

CONTENTS

INTRODUCTION

All around the world rice is eaten all around the clock, by the rich and the poor, the young and the old, on feast days and on fast days. Variously cooked and seasoned, it is the basic food of more than half the world.

In the United States, Southerners cook it wonderfully well and often. They seem to be born knowing how to achieve the dry flaky rice that is the basis for New Orleans jambalayas and pilafs, for Charleston pilaus, for rich and filling gumbos, for batter cakes—as good for breakfast with café au lait as they are in the late afternoon with a glass of cold dry white wine—for muffins, bread with a fascinating translucency, spoonbread, fritters, red beans and rice, and so on.

Northerners often seem to get panicky about cooking rice, to think there is a secret and magic formula for preparing this simple food. For these timid ones, the new precooked rice (the same idea was used in India two thousand years ago) is best, and for them many recipes using that are given in this book. With a little practice and assurance, you may use all kinds of rice interchangeably in most of the recipes in this book, according to individual preference.

Elsewhere, the warm countries—Spain, Italy, Egypt, the Near East, the Far East, and much of Latin America—and many of the colder countries—such as the Scandinavian nations, Russia, Austria, and France—have adapted rice to their ways of cooking and eating. These ways range from the rich and spectacular ceremony of the Dutch East Indies rijsttafel with twenty-four accompanying dishes, each served by a different boy, to a simple and almost parsimonious bowl of Greek lemon-and-rice soup.

The names of the many dishes in the many lands make a lovely litany, a chant for gourmets. There is mulligatawny, kedgeree, jagasee, babotee, paella, pilau, pilaf, pulao, calas, risi pisi, rijsttafel, rizogalo, nassi goreng, and crème de riz.

A linguist or a student of the migrations of peoples might be able to explain how rice cooked with broth and a little fat, with sundry bits of meat or seafood and vegetable added to it, is a pilaf in Louisiana, Egypt, the Balkans, Russia, and some countries of the Near East; but a pilau in South Carolina, Iran, and other countries of the Near East; a paella in Spain and South America; and pulao in India—all with few variations except in the seasonings. And in Italy the same thing is a risotto; but, cooked with just fresh green peas, it is risi pisi in Austria and Hungary. A rice pudding in Greece is rizogalo; the smorgasbord of the East Indies is rijsttafel. Such disparate peoples as the Swedish, inhabitants of the various Balkan countries, and the Russians all make tidy rolls of cabbage leaves with rice and meat filling, although they serve them in different sauces. The affinity between rice and dried legumes is shown in the Southern and Caribbean red beans and rice; the black beans and rice served in Tampa; the dried green peas and rice of Nassau; the black-eyed peas and rice that is called Hopping John in the Southern United States; rice with tiny orange Egyptian lentils that turn to saffron yellow when cooked, which is kedgeree; rice with dried lima beans, called jagasee; and the purée of split peas that, mixed with rice, surrounds a Hungarian pot roast.

Rice is all things to all meals—except, I insist stubbornly (despite some reputable opposition), salads. What other food may be served at breakfast (in griddle cakes, muffins, breads); in soup; in a light dish such as an egg pilau or arancini di mozzarella; in main meat dishes (Greek meat balls, jambalayas, and lots more); in curries, stuffing, vegetable dishes as pretty as the green peas and rice in risi pisi; in cheese and rice balls as a hot hors d'oeuvre to nibble with cocktails; and in such desserts as baked apples in rice custard, an ambrosial concoction of crushed raspberries, or rice and whipped cream? Rice can also be served as a wine—the Japanese *sake*—and at weddings in many countries it is thrown at the bride and groom to insure them fertility.

Rice is inexpensive, easy to store, and needs no fussy or tedious preparations. Some of the simplest ways of cooking rice are best of all. As a vegetable accompaniment, put 1 cup raw unwashed rice in a pot with 2 cups of beef or chicken bouillon, ½ teaspoon salt (most bouillon is salty, so check carefully), and 1 small onion finely chopped. Cook according to basic directions until the bouillon is absorbed, and serve with a lump of butter on top. The rice will have an almost elusive flavor from the bouillon, and the partially cooked bits of onion give a nice textural contrast to the rice.

A bowl of hot or cold flaky rice served with heavy cream and brown sugar is good for either breakfast or dessert. For the best breakfast of all, wonderfully rich and wantonly extravagant—unless there is some wild rice inexplicably left from dinner—serve a bowl of cooked wild rice with heavy cream and maple syrup.

And for a meal that will startle your guests and yet please them after they have recovered from the initial shock, serve hot wild rice with cold red caviar, quarters of hard-cooked eggs, quartered lemons, Major Grey's chutney, and salted, chilled cucumber sticks.

There is a certain gastronomic wear and tear on one's family, friends, and colleagues during the writing of a cookbook. On some there has been more burden than on others, and to them I am especially grateful—Clifford Phillips, Elisabeth Fairer, Winifred Saunders, Jean Lapolla, Helmut Ripperger, and Horace Coward.

MARIAN TRACY

THE EAST-WEST BOOK OF RICE COOKERY

1. HOW TO COOK RICE

There are many elaborate and confusing rules for cooking rice—from some rather astounding Near East ones where the rice is soaked overnight and then hung in a bag in a huge kettle of boiling water and cooked for hours, to the simpler ones used in different regions of the United States. Many good recipes may be found in basic cookbooks or on rice cartons. These are the least apt to go wrong. For convenience, some basic and reliable rules are given here.

The usual fluffy white rice, brown rice, or precooked rice may be used interchangeably in any of the recipes in this book. Different varieties are mentioned in different places, just to show the flexibility of the kinds of rice, but if you prefer one kind—or a particular way of cooking it—follow your preference in any of the recipes. Wild rice, naturally, is not quite so adaptable in its uses, but it may be used in many dishes—if somewhat expensively.

FLUFFY WHITE RICE

Put 1 cup of uncooked rice, 2 cups of cold water, and 1 teaspoon of salt in a 2-quart saucepan. Bring to a vigorous boil, cover, and then turn the heat as low as possible and cook for 14 minutes. Turn off the heat, lift the grains gently with a fork, and allow the rice to steam. The water should be all absorbed, and the grains separated, flaky, and tender, with some firmness. For extra tender grains, allow the rice to steam off the heat for 5 minutes before removing the lid. One cup of ordinary white rice makes 3 to 4 cups cooked rice.

BROWN RICE

Cook for 40 minutes, by the same method as that used for white rice.

PRECOOKED RICE

Precooked rice is even simpler to prepare than ordinary uncooked rice. Place 1⅓ cups (1 package) precooked rice in a saucepan. Add 1½ cups cold water and ½ teaspoon salt. Mix just until all rice is moistened. Bring quickly to a boil over high heat, uncovered, fluffing rice gently once or twice with a fork—do *not* stir. Cover and remove from heat. Let stand 10 minutes before serving. Makes 3 cups, or 4 to 5 servings.

WILD RICE

Wash 1 cup of wild rice repeatedly, until the water is clear. Place in a pan, cover with hot water, add 1 teaspoon of salt, and simmer over a very low heat until the rice is flaky and dry—about 40 to 60 minutes. Drain if necessary, but the water should have cooked away. One cup of wild rice makes 3 cups of cooked rice.

2. HORS D'OEUVRES AND SOUPS

PIROSHKI
WITH MEAT AND RICE FILLING
Russia

Time: 1 hour

1 batch pie dough, made according to your favorite recipe or from a prepared mix
1 large onion, minced fine
3 tablespoons butter
¾ lb. ground beef, or 2 cups chopped cooked roast beef
3 tablespoons sour cream
½ teaspoon Worcestershire sauce
½ cup cooked rice
2 tablespoons finely chopped parsley
salt, pepper
2 hard-cooked eggs, chopped

Sauté the chopped onion in butter. Stir in the beef and brown for five minutes or more. Remove from heat and add sour cream, Worcestershire sauce, rice, parsley, salt and pepper. Allow to cool, then add the chopped eggs. Pinch off pieces of pie dough the size of an egg, pat each out to an oval ¼ inch thick. Put a tablespoon of filling on each. Fold over the edges to make small finger-shaped rolls, plump in the middle with tapering ends. Place on cooky sheet and bake in 400° oven for 15 minutes, or fry in deep fat at 375° to 385°.

RICE AND CHEESE BALLS

This quantity sounds extra lavish, but it is barely enough for a moderate-sized cocktail party—of, say, twenty-five people—that is successful.

Time: 3 hours

1 package (1⅓ cups) pre-cooked rice
3 tablespoons butter
3 tablespoons flour
1 cup milk
1 teaspoon salt
dash of pepper
dash of cayenne
½ teaspoon dry mustard

1½ cups finely grated sharp cheese
¼ teaspoon Worcestershire sauce
1 teaspoon grated onion
2 egg yolks, beaten
fine breadcrumbs
fat for frying

Cook rice as directed on the package. Meanwhile, melt butter in saucepan. Add flour, blending well. Then add milk gradually, stirring constantly. Add salt, pepper, and cayenne, and cook and stir over low heat until very thick. Add mustard, cheese, Worcestershire sauce, and onion, and blend well. Then add rice and mix thoroughly. Chill.

Shape chilled mixture into 1-inch balls (approximately 1½ teaspoons each). Dip each ball in egg and fine crumbs. Fry in hot fat until golden brown on all sides. Drain on absorbent paper. Serve piping hot. Makes 85 balls.

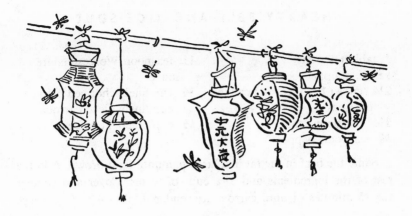

SUSHI
Japan

These are Japanese equivalents of canapés—a portable food, sometimes used, like sandwiches, to take on brief outings. Traditionally these cakes are square, but without a special mold this is a bit difficult for the inexperienced to do.

Time: 1 hour

1 cup uncooked rice
salt
pinch of sugar
4 or 5 drops vinegar

1 teaspoon horseradish (optional)
anchovies or cold cooked fish or shellfish, for garnish

Cook the rice according to basic instructions, seasoning with salt, sugar, vinegar, and horseradish if desired. Allow to cool and press into little round cakes, using a large, shallow, well-oiled muffin tin for this purpose. Unmold and decorate each cake with a bit of boiled or poached fish, a cooked shrimp, a rolled anchovy with a caper in the center—or "what have you." Makes 2 to 4 servings.

HEARTY BEEF AND RICE SOUP

Time: ½ hour

1 tablespoon fat
½ lb. chopped beef
2¼ cups (1 No. 2. can) canned tomatoes
1½ teaspoons salt
⅛ teaspoon pepper

½ teaspoon Worcestershire sauce
½ cup finely chopped onion
¾ cup finely diced carrots
½ cup precooked rice

Sauté the beef in the fat in a large pan until light brown. Add the rest of the ingredients and 2½ cups of water. Cover and simmer for 25 minutes or until carrots are tender. Makes 4 to 6 servings.

CHICKEN SOUP
Armenia

Time: 25 minutes

1½ quarts well-seasoned chicken broth
¼ cup uncooked rice

1 egg, beaten
salt, pepper
juice of ½ lemon

Bring broth to a boil, add rice, and simmer until tender, about 20 minutes. Salt and pepper the egg and add the lemon juice slowly, stirring well. Just before serving, stir the lemon and egg thickening into the hot soup. Makes 4 to 6 servings.

For a luxurious and untypical version, add ½ cup diced chicken meat. Makes 4 to 6 generous servings.

CREAM OF CHICKEN SOUP
WITH CHICKEN AND ALMONDS

This is a delicate and yet voluptuous soup, lightly sustaining, especially soothing to tortured stomachs, if you omit the almonds, but elegant enough for a special luncheon with an unusual salad and hot bread.

Time: 35 minutes

4 cups chicken broth (stock or canned—not cubes this time)
¼ cup uncooked rice
½ cup diced cooked chicken
1 tablespoon butter

½ cup almonds, blanched and slivered
2 cups cream (preferably heavy)
salt, pepper, if necessary

Simmer the rice and chicken in the broth for 20 to 30 minutes. Meanwhile, sauté the almonds in butter. Add the cream to the broth and simmer for 2 or 3 minutes, just long enough for the flavors to become casually acquainted. Add seasonings, if necessary. Serve in small warmed soup bowls with some of the almonds in each bowl. Makes 4 servings.

MULLIGATAWNY
India

This traditional Indian curried soup may be made with rabbit instead of chicken.

Time: 2½ hours

1 3- to 4-lb. fowl
4 tablespoons butter
1 onion, minced
2 apples, minced
1 tablespoon flour
8 cups chicken or veal stock (or water)
1½ teaspoons curry powder

4 tablespoons tomato paste
½ green pepper, minced
1 teaspoon sugar
2 cloves
¼ teaspoon mace
4 tablespoons grated coconut
½ cup boiled rice

Cut up the chicken and brown in the butter in a Dutch oven or soup pot. Remove and reserve. Brown onion and apples in the same butter, sprinkle with flour, and gradually stir in the stock. Add all the seasonings, the green pepper, coconut, tomato paste, and the chicken, and simmer for 2 hours. Remove chicken, strain the soup, forcing as much of the pulp as possible through a fine sieve. Return the chicken to the soup and serve in warmed bowls, with a tablespoon of rice in each bowl. Makes 6 to 8 servings.

FISH SOUP
Russia

In the authentic Russian and Siberian versions, the soup is strained before adding the rice and shrimp, but Americans may prefer to simplify the making by leaving the vegetables and fish in. It is traditional to serve a dish of chopped scallions on the side and sprinkle a few in each bowl.

Time: 1½ hours

2 lbs. white fish—cod, haddock, or flounder—cut in pieces
½ cup diced celery
2 leeks, quartered and then cut in 1-inch pieces
⅓ cup chopped parsley
1 clove garlic, minced
6 to 8 peppercorns
dash of nutmeg
salt
¼ cup uncooked rice
¼ cup fresh cooked shrimp, peeled and cleaned, or 1 small can shrimp
2 tablespoons white wine (nice but not obligatory)

Put the fish, celery, leeks, parsley, garlic, peppercorns, salt, and the merest pinch of nutmeg in a pan with 6 cups water. Cover and simmer for at least 1 hour. (The fish will be cooked before this, but the flavor improves with long simmering.) Strain—or don't— and put back in pan; add uncooked rice. Simmer for about 15 minutes or until rice is tender. Add shrimps and simmer for about 5 minutes more. Just before serving, add wine. Makes 4 servings.

LOUISIANA GUMBO

All gumbos, no matter how else they vary, have okra or filé powder or both as ingredients.

Time: 45 minutes

3 tablespoons butter
½ cup chopped onion
½ cup chopped green pepper
½ cup chopped celery
1 clove garlic, finely chopped
¾ cup sliced okra
2 cups canned tomatoes
1½ cups chicken broth
1 teaspoon sugar

dash of pepper
pinch of thyme
small piece of bay leaf
½ lb. uncooked shrimp, peeled
   and de-veined
½ pint oysters
1 package (1⅓ cups) pre-
   cooked rice
½ teaspoon salt

Sauté the onion, green pepper, celery, and garlic in the butter in a heavy and deep skillet until lightly browned. Add the okra, tomatoes, broth, and all seasonings except the salt. Cover and simmer for about ½ hour, stirring occasionally. Meanwhile, mix the pre-cooked rice with 1½ cups of water and the salt, and cook according to the directions on the package. After the gumbo has simmered for ½ hour, add the shrimp. Cook for 5 minutes. Add the oysters and cook just until their edges curl. Put a large spoonful of rice in each soup bowl of gumbo. Makes 5 or 6 servings.

SHRIMP GUMBO

Time: 1½ hours

1 tablespoon bacon fat
1 bunch of spring onions—chop the bottoms and save the tops
2 cups fresh okra, sliced
1 cup peeled and chopped tomatoes, or 1 cup canned tomatoes
4 cups stock or bouillon
1 hot red pepper pod
1 green pepper, chopped and seeds removed
1 bay leaf
pinch of thyme
salt
1 lb. shrimp, cooked, peeled, and cleaned
1 tablespoon filé powder
½ cup cooked rice, or more

Melt the bacon fat in a pan and sauté the onion bottoms with the okra for about ten minutes. Add the stock, tomatoes, peppers, onion tops cut in pieces, and all seasonings except for the filé powder. Bring to a boil and then simmer over a low flame for 10 minutes. Add the shrimp, cover pan tightly, and simmer for about 1 hour. Just before serving add the filé powder, which is a seasoning and a thickening but must never be cooked. Serve with a little boiled rice in each soup bowl. Makes 4 to 6 servings.

RICE AND LEMON SOUP
Balkans

Time: 15 minutes

4 cups (1 quart) chicken or
  veal consommé
3 tablespoons cooked rice

4 thin slices lemon
2 tablespoons minced parsley

Add rice to consommé and cook gently for 10 minutes. Add lemon slices, but do not let boil. Let stand 3 or 4 minutes before serving in cups. Sprinkle with parsley. Makes 4 servings.

TOMATO BOUILLON WITH RICE

One-third cup of uncooked rice to one quart of liquid is a good proportion in consommé, bouillon, broth, or any clear soup cooked with rice.

Time: 20 minutes

2 cups consommé
2 cups tomato juice

salt, pepper
⅓ cup precooked rice

Mix the consommé and tomato juice in a saucepan. Add salt and pepper. Add precooked rice. Bring to a boil and simmer 10 to 15 minutes. Serve at once. Makes 4 to 6 servings.

YOGHURT SOUP

Armenia

Time: ½ hour

1 onion, sliced thin
1 tablespoon butter
4 cups beef broth or bouillon (homemade, canned, or made from cubes)
⅓ cup uncooked rice

1 slice lemon
⅔ cup yoghurt
salt and pepper
fresh mint and parsley, chopped fine

Sauté the onion in the butter until pale yellow but still crisp. Meanwhile, simmer the rice and the lemon in the bouillon for 10 minutes and add sautéed onion. Continue simmering for 10 more minutes. Before serving, stir some of the hot soup into the yoghurt. When the mixture is smooth, add the remainder of the soup. Stir over lowest possible heat until mixture is smooth and creamy and yoghurt is just hot but not cooked. Season, remove from the heat, and let cool slightly before serving. Sprinkle each bowl of soup with mint and parsley. Makes 4 servings.

CURRIED CONSOMMÉ

A good prelude to a large cold seafood salad on a hot day.

Time: 1 hour

2 tablespoons butter
1 large onion, chopped
2 slices bacon, cut in pieces
1 tablespoon flour
1 tablespoon curry powder
(more or less, according to
taste)

5 cups bouillon (stock, canned,
or cubes)
⅓ cup uncooked rice
⅓ cup finely chopped parsley
⅓ cup freshly grated Parmesan
cheese

Sauté the onion and bacon briefly in the butter. Sprinkle with the flour and curry powder. Blend well and add the bouillon and rice. Simmer for at least an hour to get the best flavor. Serve in warm bowls and sprinkle with parsley and Parmesan cheese. Makes 4 servings.

RICE PORRIDGE
Denmark

This is a Danish Christmas dish, served just before the roast goose at dinner. The almond is placed in one of the plates. According to Danish legend, the person who gets the almond will be married during the next year.

Time: 1¾ hours

¾ cup uncooked rice
2 quarts milk

3 or more tablespoons butter
1 whole almond

Wash the rice well, and scald it. Bring the milk to a boil and stir in the rice. Simmer over a low flame for an hour and a half, adding more hot milk if the porridge seems too dry. Add butter and stir until melted. Makes 6 to 8 generous servings.

CREAM OF RICE SOUP

This classic soup is more than just smooth, bland, and gentle. It is elegant, suitable for your most fastidious relatives.

Time: 1 hour

1 cup uncooked rice	2 egg yolks
6 cups veal or chicken broth	salt
1 cup heavy cream	white pepper

Wash rice in several waters and drain well. Simmer in 4 cups of veal or chicken broth until rice is very tender—about 45 to 50 minutes. Force through a fine sieve, season, and dilute with 2 cups of broth. Beat the egg yolks, stir in the cream, and then stir in a bit of the hot soup. Add the resulting mixture to the rest of the soup; reheat, but do not permit to boil, lest it curdle. Makes 6 generous servings.

3. CURRIES

Despite the usual American conception, true curries are not floury cream sauces flavored with curry powder and masking diced leftovers. The classic way to make curry is to sauté chopped onion and a tart apple in butter that has been mixed with curry powder, then add chicken stock and coconut milk (which can be made by pouring boiling water over grated coconut) or a combination of stock and evaporated cream cooked together. A little flour is added, but not enough to make the usual cream-sauce consistency. Curry is best when the meat has been chilled in the sauce overnight to allow it to ripen, as it were. Almost any meat, except ham, can be used, and any kind of poultry or shellfish. Serve all curries with a large bowl of hot, fluffy rice, chutney, and some of the following accompaniments (in separate, tiny bowls to be passed around on a tray): chopped nuts, chopped hard-boiled eggs, chopped preserved ginger, grated orange peel, sliced bananas, chopped raw onion, grated coconut, cooked crumbled bacon, Bombay duck (an Indian dried fish).

19

A spoonful of each may be scattered over the individual plates of curry. Serve about four to six of these with one curry.

Curries need no other accompaniment except salad and perhaps some French bread. Tea tastes better with them than coffee, for some fundamental reason.

CURRY POWDER

Curry powder seems, to most people, a definite spice like cinnamon or cloves, or else a compound mixed according to a carefully guarded formula. But in India curry powder is mixed fresh for each dish and varies from household to household according to personal idiosyncrasies, and also to suit the dish it is to season.

Anyone who has a good collection of seasonings and is not timid can mix fresh curry powder. A pinch of this and a pinch of that, pounded together in a mortar with a pestle—or in a small bowl with a "blunt instrument"—will make it. After a little practice it will be easy to achieve the most individually pleasing flavor. The seasoning that gives curry its characteristic rich amber color is tumeric, so use that and add any of these seasonings in various combinations: pepper, red pepper, coriander, celery seed, ginger, cinnamon, allspice, cloves, nutmeg, cumin, fennel, cardamon, mace. Be sure to omit ginger for a seafood curry.

When you buy curry powder already mixed, choose the best brand you can find. The more expensive brands are stronger, and the difference in cost is only a few cents for a year's supply.

CHUTNEY

All curry dishes are accompanied by not only rice but chutney, a hot, spicy, fruit-and-vegetable sort of pickle. The well-known East Indian ones have mangoes as a base and are comparatively expensive to buy. But many other versions may be made at home pleasurably and easily over an otherwise leisurely weekend.

HELMUT RIPPERGER'S
GREEN TOMATO CHUTNEY

12 medium-sized green
 tomatoes
4 tablespoons salt
1½ lbs. brown sugar
6 cups cider vinegar
18 tart apples

3 medium-sized Spanish onions
½ lb. green ginger
2 hot peppers
1 bunch celery
3 cups seedless raisins
¼ cup mustard seed

Chop the tomatoes and sprinkle with 2 tablespoons salt. Let stand overnight. Drain. Dissolve the rest of the salt with the sugar in the vinegar. Chop apples, peppers, ginger, celery, and onions. Mix all together with other ingredients and cook until tender and thick—½ to ¾ of an hour. Pour into clean *hot* jars and seal immediately.

EAST INDIAN CHUTNEY

1 cup tarragon vinegar
1 cup cider vinegar
3 cups sugar
¼ cup fresh ginger root, minced
 or ground
½ lb. currants

6 cups peeled, diced, not-too-
 ripe peaches
2 cloves garlic, peeled and
 minced, ground, or mashed
1 tablespoon salt

Cook vinegar and sugar together until they form a clear sirup. Add ginger root and cook for 20 minutes. Add the rest of the ingredients and simmer, covered, over *very* low flame for about 3 hours, stirring occasionally. Put an asbestos pad under the pan in order to prevent scorching—or watch very carefully. Pour into clean, hot jars and seal.

CHERRY CHUTNEY

3 quarts cherries, washed, stemmed, and seeded
6 cups chopped onions
1 lb. currants
2 oz. preserved ginger, chopped
¼ cup mustard seed
1 tablespoon salt
3 cups sugar
2 quarts cider vinegar
1 teaspoon each cinnamon, mace, cloves, and allspice

Put all ingredients in a pan. Cover and simmer 3 hours or until thick. Pour into clean, hot jars and seal. For a better flavor, let ripen a month or two before using.

RIJSTTAFEL
East Indies

Rijsttafel is an East Indian version of a smorgasbord—a highly seasoned meal served in many separate bowls and with hot, flaky rice. Though the meat dishes are not invariably curried, as most people think, the style of serving is an outsize version of that used for any curry. It makes an unusual and spectacular arrangement for a buffet, and fits in well with American informal entertaining. The Chinese style is to put rice onto the individual plate and then layers of food from different dishes on top. In other versions, each person puts a fluffy pile of rice on a plate, chooses food from some of the dishes, and spoons it onto the plate with the rice. Following is a list of some of the dishes used in Rijsttafel.

hot cooked rice
roast chicken (carved at the
    table)
dried fish (Bombay duck)
tiny meat balls
curry sauce, or other highly
    spiced sauce
pickled peppers
chopped raw onion
chopped hard-cooked eggs

chutney
fried bananas
fried eggplant
coconut
chopped nuts
preserved ginger
finely shredded preserved
    oranges
curried lime chutney
Indian relish or other relish

CURRY

This is best with diced poultry, lamb, or seafood. Serve in its simplest form with just rice, chutney, and coconut.

Time: 45 minutes

1 tablespoon curry powder (or more for experienced palates)
1 onion, sliced
1 tart apple, diced
3 tablespoons butter
¼ cup raisins
1½ cups meat stock, seafood stock, or milk
3½ tablespoons flour
1 cup light cream or evaporated milk
salt and pepper
1½ to 2 cups diced cooked meat or seafood

Sauté curry powder, onion, and apple in butter, blending well. Add raisins and stock or milk. Mix flour and cream and stir until smooth. Add to onion and apple mixture. Stir over a low heat until thick and creamy. Season with salt and pepper. Add cooked meat or seafood. Reheat. Makes 4 to 6 servings.

FISH-AND-FOWL CURRY

This is a delicate version, particularly adaptable to chicken, turkey, shrimp, or lobster.

Time: ½ hour

1 tablespoon butter
¼ cup chopped onion
1 clove garlic
1 tablespoon flour
2 tablespoons curry powder (or more to taste)
1 teaspoon salt
½ teaspoon ginger
paprika to taste

1 cup soup stock, cream, or canned milk diluted just to the consistency of very heavy fresh cream
4 cups chopped cooked fowl or fish
1 egg, well beaten
1 tablespoon Worcestershire sauce

Melt butter in a skillet. Add onion and garlic and cook until medium brown. Remove garlic. Add flour, curry powder, and seasoning. Add soup stock or cream. Add meat and egg. Cook over very low heat, slowly, so that egg does not curdle. Let come to boil, add Worcestershire sauce, and serve immediately with rice. Makes 6 servings.

When chicken is used, this dish will be best if the chicken is boiled the day before, and its liquid is used as stock. Cut the meat from the bones, make the curry sauce, and chill the dish, uncovered, in the refrigerator, so that the flavors may ripen.

HAWAIIAN CURRY

Hawaiian Curry usually seems milder and sweeter than the Indian version. Why, I don't know, because there is the usual amount of good curry powder in it. With this dish, pass around small bowls of salted almonds or peanuts, chopped sweet onions, crisp chopped bacon, shredded coconut, and chutney. The chutney is obligatory; several of the others at a time are pleasing and traditional.

Time: 2 hours

2 tablespoons butter
2 medium-sized onions, chopped
2 tart cooking apples, peeled, cored, and diced
2 fat cloves garlic, minced
2 tablespoons curry powder
1 can Southern style moist coconut or 1 cup freshly grated coconut
2 cups milk

3 tablespoons butter, softened
3 tablespoons flour
2 cups raw chicken cut in pieces, or raw peeled and cleaned shrimp
1 cup fresh pineapple or 1 package frozen pineapple chunks (canned crushed pineapple will not do—not enough texture)

Sauté the onions, apples, and garlic in 2 tablespoons butter. Add the curry powder and stir briefly. Meanwhile soak the coconut in the milk (if the coconut is fresh, use its milk as part of the liquid). Add the milk and coconut to the sauce. Mix the softened butter and flour. Stir until smooth. Add to the pan and simmer over a low flame for about 45 minutes. Add the chicken or shrimp and simmer until tender. This dish is better if the meat stays in the sauce overnight to ripen in the refrigerator. Heat, and add the pineapple just before serving. Serve with large bowls of rice. Makes 6 servings.

RABBIT CURRY
France

There is no nonsense about this French curry. It is a fine simple and rich meat sauce, served with rice, and that's it—no accompaniments, no chutney.

Time: 2 hours

1 rabbit (about 3 lbs.), cut up for frying
flour, salt, pepper
3 tablespoons butter
1 small onion, finely chopped
½ cup white wine

1 to 1½ cups beef bouillon
1 tablespoon curry powder
2 egg yolks, beaten
⅓ cup heavy cream
salt
1½ cups rice, cooked

Shake the pieces of rabbit in a bag with flour, salt, and pepper until lightly coated. Sauté in butter until golden brown. Add the onion, white wine, and enough bouillon to cover—this will vary with the size of the rabbit and the size of the pan. Take a spoonful of the bouillon and mix with the curry powder. Add to the rabbit, cover, and simmer from 1½ to 2 hours. Transfer the pieces of rabbit to a warm platter in a warm place. Skim the fat off the liquid by brushing the top with a paper towel. Take a spoonful of the liquid and mix with the beaten egg yolks and heavy cream. Add to the juices in the bottom of the pan and stir until smooth. Add more seasoning if necessary. Cook a minute or two until well mingled and then pour over the rabbit. Serve with a bowl of fluffy hot rice. Makes 4 servings.

LAMB CURRY

Good, uncomplicated, but *not* dull.

Time: 1½ hours

2¼ lbs. boned lamb shoulder
½ cup finely chopped onions
2 tablespoons fat
2½ teaspoons salt
¼ teaspoon pepper

2 tablespoons flour
2½ teaspoons curry powder
2 teaspoons vinegar
1 package (1⅓ cups) pre-cooked rice

Remove fat and gristle from lamb. Then cut meat in 1¼-inch cubes. Sauté lamb and onions in hot fat in heavy saucepan or skillet until lightly browned. Add 2 teaspoons salt, pepper, and 2 cups of water. Simmer, covered, 1 hour, or until meat is tender. Add 3 more cups of water and reheat. Blend flour with ½ cup water. Add gradually to lamb mixture, stirring constantly until thickened. Add curry powder and vinegar. Cook rice with ½ teaspoon salt, according to directions on the package. Arrange rice on hot platter, cover with curry mixture, and serve at once. Makes 6 servings.

LAMB CURRY WITH BANANAS
West Indies

Curry in the West Indies is usually served with only sautéed bananas to mitigate the fiery flavor of the curry—no multiple accompaniments as in the Indian or Hawaiian kinds.

Time: 1 hour

¼ teaspoon saffron
1 cup uncooked rice
3 tablespoons olive oil or butter
1 medium-sized onion, sliced thin
1 small clove garlic, chopped fine
½ green pepper, seeds removed, chopped fine
2 tablespoons flour
2 cups rich meat stock or bouillon
½ cup strained canned tomatoes or peeled, seeded, chopped fresh tomatoes

1 large bay leaf
8 pieces fresh parsley
1 pinch thyme
2 whole cloves
dash of ground mace
salt, pepper
2 tablespoons curry powder (more or less, according to individual tolerance)
2½ to 3 cups cooked lamb, cut in small cubes
3 not quite ripe bananas, sliced about ½ inch thick, lengthwise

Dissolve the saffron in ¼ cup water. Add to the rice, and cook the rice in water according to basic directions. Sauté the onion, garlic, and green pepper in 2 tablespoons butter or oil until golden brown. Sprinkle the flour on top. Stir until well blended and add the meat stock or bouillon. Simmer until thick and smooth. Add the tomatoes and seasonings and simmer until the sauce is thick and somewhat smooth again. Dump in the cubed lamb and let stand in the sauce—preferably overnight but at least an hour. Meanwhile sauté the banana slices in 1 tablespoon butter or oil. Heat the lamb very briefly, just long enough to get it really hot. Pour over the hot rice piled on a warm platter, surround with the banana slices, and serve immediately. Makes 4 to 6 servings.

COUNTRY CAPTAIN

This is a famous English-Indian dish which somehow found its way to the South and is included in most collections of Southern recipes. The Indian version, given below, is simpler. To make the Southern, add a large can of tomatoes, chopped celery, and green pepper to the sauce while the chicken is simmering in it.

Time: 1 hour

¼ cup olive oil
2 cloves garlic, peeled and cut in half
2 medium-sized onions, sliced thin
1 3½-lb. frying chicken, cut up for frying
flour
salt
3 cups chicken stock or chicken bouillon made from cubes

1 tablespoon good curry powder, more or less, according to taste
⅓ cup blanched almonds
2 tablespoons butter
3 tablespoons currants (or white seedless grapes— neither Indian nor Southern, but a good variant anyway)
2 cups rice, cooked dry and flaky

Sauté the garlic and onion in oil until translucent. Remove. Flour and salt the pieces of chicken and fry in the oil in a heavy deep skillet or Dutch oven until golden brown. Add the garlic, onion, stock, and curry powder. Cover and simmer 45 minutes or until meat is tender. Brown the almonds in the butter. Pile the chicken in the center of a warm platter, surround with hot, cooked rice mixed lightly with currants. Remove the garlic from the sauce in the chicken pan and pour the sauce over the chicken and rice. Sprinkle the almonds over all. Makes 4 servings.

CURRIED CHICKEN

This recipe, adapted from the one used at the Hotel Pierre in New York, is best served with Saffron Rice (see index) and such accompaniments as chutney, coconut, slivered almonds, and grated orange rind.

Time: 3 hours

½ cup butter
1½ cups chopped onions
3 or 4 cloves garlic, minced
1½ bay leaves
1 teaspoon cinnamon
5 or 6 whole cloves
1 5-lb. fowl, cut in pieces for stewing

1½ tablespoons salt
1 teaspoon black pepper
1 teaspoon cumin
1 teaspoon coriander
1 tablespoon paprika
2 tablespoons curry powder
2 medium-sized tomatoes, quartered

Melt butter in a large saucepan. Add onions and garlic, and sauté until tender. Add bay leaves, cinnamon, and cloves. Cover and simmer 5 minutes. Add chicken, and cook uncovered until chicken begins to dry out. Add salt, pepper, cumin, coriander, paprika, and curry powder. Stir carefully. Add tomatoes and 6 cups water. Cover and cook 2 to 2½ hours, or until chicken is tender. Remove chicken meat from bones and cut meat into 1-inch pieces. Skim fat from broth; add chicken. Thicken broth if desired. Makes 8 servings.

PULAO
India

This is an unusual and fine dish for a buffet supper. It is unlike most curries in that the meat predominates. Serve with chutney and a bland salad—say, sliced avocado with a bitter and exotic green like Belgian endive. Follow with a chilled half-watermelon scooped out slightly and piled high with watermelon balls, cante-loupe balls, fresh strawberries, and white grapes. (In India buffalo butter—ghee—is used to sauté the onions—but try to get some at your corner grocery store.)

Time: 1½ hours

3 onions, chopped (keep 1 separate for garnish)
1 cup butter or peanut oil
2 fricassee chickens (3 lbs. each), cut up
flour, salt, pepper
2 cups uncooked rice

3 teaspoons curry powder, or more
1 tablespoon chopped ginger (green or preserved)
1 cup seeded raisins
1 cup blanched almonds

Sauté 2 chopped onions in the butter until soft, and then remove and reserve. Put the pieces of chicken in a paper bag with flour, salt, and pepper; shake well until each piece is coated. Brown the chicken in the same fat in which the onions were cooked. Put the chickens, sautéed onions, and 1 cup water in a large pot and simmer about 1 hour or more, until the meat is tender. In the meantime, cook the rice (see basic instructions), with the curry powder and salt.

When the chicken is cooked, remove the meat from the bones, leaving it in large pieces. Add to the rice, with the ginger, raisins, and almonds. Make into a mound on an ovenproof dish, pour the broth in which the chicken was cooked over all, and keep warm (but not too long) in a medium oven. When ready to serve, sprinkle with chopped onion, either raw or lightly fried. Serve with chutney. Makes 10 servings.

JAN KINDLER'S CURRY
WITH CAPONATINA

Caponatina is an Italian eggplant relish that comes in tiny cans and is sold almost everywhere. Its spiciness gives somewhat the same emphasis and contrast to the curry as chutney, but it is much less expensive—about 18 cents a can.

Time: 40 minutes

6 tablespoons butter, or more
⅓ cup blanched almonds
½ lb. mushrooms, sliced
2 onions, chopped
1 buffet-size can caponatina
1 small can small green peas, drained

1 cup diced cooked pork or chicken
2 tablespoons diced pimiento
1 tablespoon curry powder or more
salt
1½ cups hot cooked brown rice

Sauté the almonds, mushrooms, and onions separately in butter. Mix all ingredients except the rice, and simmer for 15 minutes or more. Mound the rice on a platter and spoon the caponatina mixture on top. Makes 3 or 4 servings.

LOBSTER CURRY

This is delicate and simple, needing only rice, chutney, and almonds for perfection.

Time: 1 hour

3 tablespoons butter or cooking oil
2 medium-sized onions, chopped
1 fat or 2 small cloves garlic, chopped fine
1 tablespoon curry powder (more if taste permits)
1 lemon, juice and grated peel

1 lb. lobster meat, pulled apart, and membranes removed
1 cup coconut milk (fresh, or made by pouring 1 cup boiling water over ½ cup grated coconut) or evaporated milk with a good texture
salt, pepper

Sauté the onion and garlic in the butter or oil until pale yellow. Add the curry powder, blend in well, and then add the grated lemon peel and juice. Cook until smooth, add the lobster, coconut milk, and salt and pepper. Simmer over an infinitesimal flame for 50 to 60 minutes. Makes 4 servings.

BILL MOORE'S OYSTER CURRY

This concoction, created by an able naval captain, deviates somewhat from the basic rules, but with pleasing results. Serve with hot,
fluffy rice, and pass little bowls of chopped raw onion, chutney,
grated egg yolks, and crisp crumbled bacon to be sprinkled on each
serving.

Time: 20 minutes

1 pint oysters, and their liquor	milk
3 tablespoons butter	1½ teaspoons curry powder
3 tablespoons flour	salt

Heat the oysters in their liquor until the edges curl. Reserve
oysters and keep warm. Add milk to oyster liquor to make 2 cups
of liquid. Make a cream sauce by blending the butter and flour
until smooth and adding the milk-and-oyster-liquor mixture, stirring
until smooth and thick. When the sauce has thickened, add salt and
curry powder. Add the oysters and serve. Makes 2 to 4 servings.

NASSI GORENG
Java

A Javanese mishmash of fried rice and whatever is in the house.

Time: 45 minutes

¼ cup butter
2 tablespoons curry powder
1 cup uncooked rice
salt, pepper
1 cup, or more, chicken broth
1 cup chopped, parboiled or partly cooked celery and onion

1 cup shrimp, peeled and cleaned
½ cup diced ham, veal, chicken livers, or tiny meat balls
cucumber, peeled and sliced lengthwise, or a fried egg for each portion, as garnish

Melt the butter, add curry powder, and stir until you have a smooth, spicy blend. Add the rice and stir again until each grain is coated and covered. Add salt, pepper, and chicken broth. Cover and transfer to the oven; cook until the rice is tender and flaky. Add celery and onion, shrimp, and bits of meat. Heat just long enough to get really hot. Top each serving with sliced cucumber or fried egg. Makes 4 servings.

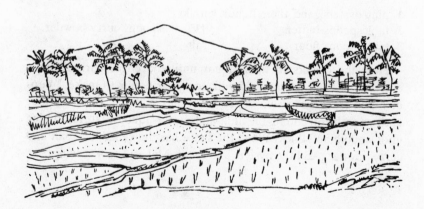

CURRIED RICE

Good served with shrimp, crabmeat, any kind of lamb, or roast beef.

Time: 25 minutes

2 tablespoons butter
1 large onion, chopped
1 package (1⅓ cups) pre-cooked rice

1 teaspoon curry powder (or more according to taste)
¾ teaspoon salt

Melt butter in saucepan, add onion and rice, and sauté over low heat until rice is golden brown, stirring constantly. Add curry powder, salt, and 1½ cups water. Mix just until all rice is moistened. Bring quickly to a boil over high heat, uncovered, fluffing rice gently once or twice with a fork (do *not* stir). Boil 2 to 3 minutes. Cover and remove from heat. Let stand 10 minutes. Makes 4 servings.

4. MEAT

GREEK MEAT BALLS

These may also be served without the sauce as an unusual hot hors d'oeuvre. Supply toothpicks for convenience in picking up the hot morsels.

Time: 50 minutes

1½ lbs. ground beef
⅓ cup uncooked rice
½ cup canned tomatoes
1 large onion, chopped fine
3 tablespoons finely chopped
    parsley
salt, pepper

2 eggs, beaten
6 cups bouillon (or salted water
    with sliced lemon)

SAUCE

2 eggs, beaten
juice of 1 lemon

Mix all ingredients except the bouillon, in order given, kneading after the eggs are added. Roll into small balls about 1 to 1½ inches in diameter. Bring bouillon or salted water to a boil, and drop meat balls in. Cover and cook for 20 to 30 minutes. The balls are done when they come to the top.

Serve with an egg-and-lemon sauce made by adding to the beaten eggs first the lemon juice and then 1 tablespoon of the broth the meat balls were cooked in. Makes 4 to 6 servings as meat course of a meal.

BABOTEE
South Africa

A Dutch-African farm dish, a sort of curried meat custard served with rice and chutney.

Time: 1 hour

4 tablespoons butter
1 onion, chopped fine
1½ lbs. chopped cooked meat
1 slice of bread soaked in the juices from the cooked meat
½ cup blanched and slivered almonds

1 tablespoon curry powder
juice of 1 lemon
grated peel of ½ lemon
salt, pepper
2 eggs, beaten
1 cup milk, scalded
1 bay leaf

Melt the butter, sauté the onion, and add to the meat. Crumble the bread and mix in. Add almonds, curry powder, lemon juice, grated lemon peel, and seasoning. Mix thoroughly and put in shallow buttered casserole. Add scalded milk and crumbled bay leaf to the beaten eggs, and pour over the meat. Put casserole in pan with about an inch of water, and bake in a moderate oven (350°) until the custard is firm, or a knife inserted comes out clean—about 30 minutes. Serve with chutney and boiled rice. Makes 4 servings.

STUFFED FLANK STEAK

Time: 2¼ hours

2 cups cooked rice
½ stick butter, melted
⅓ cup finely chopped parsley
paprika
1 flank steak (about 1½ lbs.)
salt
freshly ground black pepper
2 tablespoons bacon drippings
  or other fat
½ cup tomato juice
1 tablespoon Worcestershire
  sauce

Mix the rice with melted butter, parsley, and a dash of paprika. Use a rolling pin or bottle to pound the steak until thin. Sprinkle with salt and freshly ground black pepper and spread the rice mixture evenly over it. Roll the steak up and tie with string or secure with poultry skewers. Brown on all sides in the fat in a Dutch oven. Add tomato juice, Worcestershire sauce, and about 2 cups of water. Cover and bake in 350° oven for about 2 hours or until the meat is tender. Makes 6 servings.

PLAIN AMERICAN

Something you can put together the night it's raining torrents and you don't want to shop—assuming that your refrigerator is well stocked.

Time: 1 hour

1 lb. chopped beef
1 small onion, minced
1 cup soft breadcrumbs
⅓ cup milk
1 egg, beaten
1 teaspoon Worcestershire sauce
1 teaspoon salt

pepper
2 tablespoons bacon fat
1 can bouillon
1 small can tomato sauce
¼ lb. fresh mushrooms, sliced
¼ cup uncooked rice
1 package frozen lima beans
juice of ½ lemon

Mix chopped beef, onion, crumbs, milk, egg, Worcestershire sauce, and seasoning. Form into balls. Sauté the meat balls in bacon fat in heavy skillet. Add bouillon, 1½ cups water, and tomato sauce. Cover and simmer ½ hour. Add mushrooms, rice, and lima beans. Cook until they are tender, which will be about 20 minutes more. Add lemon juice. Makes 4 servings.

CHILI RICE

This is one of those nice naturalized-American dishes adapted to whatever is on hand.

Time: 20 minutes

2 tablespoons butter
1 lb. ground beef
1 large onion, chopped
1 package (1⅓ cups) pre-cooked rice

1 cup chili sauce
1½ teaspoons chili powder
2 teaspoons salt
freshly ground black pepper
1 buffet-size can kidney beans

Melt butter in a large skillet and sauté beef and onion until brown. Add the rice, 1½ cups boiling water, chili sauce, and seasonings. (This amount of chili powder is for the average taste—addicts will like more.) Cover and simmer 10 minutes. Add beans and simmer for 3 or 4 minutes or until beans are hot. Makes 6 servings.

STUFFED PEPPERS

Time: 45 minutes

6 green peppers
½ onion, minced
4 tablespoons butter
1 cup boiled rice

1 cup minced cooked meat
(ham, lamb, veal, or beef)
salt, pepper
2 cups tomato juice

Seed, wash, and rinse the peppers thoroughly. Sauté the minced onion in 2 tablespoons butter, add the rice and meat and seasoning and mix well. Stuff the peppers with this mixture. Then brown them slightly in 2 tablespoons of butter. Stand them upright in a pot—if possible—pour juice around them, and simmer for 20 to 30 minutes, or until the peppers can easily be pierced with a fork. Makes 6 servings.

ZUCCHINI STUFFED WITH RICE
IN TOMATO SAUCE

Zucchini stuffed with rice, Italian fashion, is quite different from the Balkan versions of stuffed vegetables.

Time: 1¼ hours

8 zucchini, each about 6 inches long
2 tablespoons butter or olive oil
1 medium-sized onion, chopped
½ lb. beef round, chopped

⅓ cup uncooked rice
salt, pepper
4 medium-sized tomatoes, peeled, quartered, and seeds pressed out
2 tablespoons olive oil

Cut each zucchini into three pieces and hollow out the center with an apple corer. Sauté the chopped onion and beef briefly in the butter. Mix with uncooked rice, salt, and pepper. Arrange the pieces of zucchini on end in a casserole. Fill the holes with the meat mixture. Pour about ½ inch water around the zucchini and arrange the pieces of tomatoes around and in between. Salt and pepper them and sprinkle with two tablespoons of olive oil. Bake in a slow (300°) oven 45 to 60 minutes or until the zucchini is tender and the tomatoes have thickened into a sauce. Serve in the dish. Makes 4 servings.

GOLUBSKY
Russia

From the Balkans to the Scandinavian countries, you will find in homes and restaurants tidy packages of rice and meat wrapped in cabbage leaves. The seasonings and the sauce or gravy served with them vary from country to country. This is the Russian version, particularly pleasing with its spicy and unctuous tomato and sour cream sauce.

Time: 1 hour

12 cabbage leaves
¼ lb. chopped pork
1 onion, chopped
⅓ cup butter
¼ lb. chopped beef
¼ lb. chopped veal
1 egg

1½ cups cooked rice
salt, pepper
1 cup tomato juice
1 tablespoon Italian tomato
   paste
⅔ cup sour cream

Drop the cabbage leaves in boiling water for a minute or two (not longer) to make them pliable. Let them drain. Sauté the pork and onion in half the butter for about 10 minutes. Remove from fire, cool slightly, and mix with beef, veal, the egg, rice, and seasoning. Mix thoroughly and divide the mixture into 12 portions and put one on each cabbage leaf. Roll up the leaves and put side by side in the same heavy skillet that was used for the onion and pork, adding more butter. Brown on one side and then turn over, being careful not to let bundles come undone. Brown on that side, cover, and cook over very low flame for 30 to 40 minutes.

Transfer carefully from the pan to a hot platter, and keep warm. Add the tomato juice and tomato paste to the juices in the pan. Stir around until smooth. When well mingled, add the sour cream and blend well. Simmer over very low flame for 5 minutes. Taste and season if necessary—some tomato juice has plenty of seasoning. Pour over the cabbage rolls. Makes 4 servings.

VEAL IN SAUTERNE SAUCE
WITH HEARTS OF ARTICHOKES
AND WILD RICE

Time: 45 minutes

1½ lbs. veal cutlet, cut thin, as
    for scallopine
3 tablespoons butter or other fat
2 tablespoons flour
1 cup chicken broth or bouillon
½ cup sauterne

salt, pepper
½ teaspoon dried marjoram
1 small (8-oz.) can hearts
    of artichokes, drained
2 cups cooked wild rice

Sauté the veal in butter or fat until golden brown, then remove
and blend in the flour, chicken broth, sauterne, and seasonings until
the sauce is thick and smooth. Spread the rice in a casserole and
scatter the hearts of artichokes on top. Place the veal cutlets on
top, and pour the sauce over all. Bake in a 350° oven 20 minutes
or until flavors are intermingled. Makes 4 servings.

BAKED SLICED CALVES' HEARTS
WITH RICE

Time: 1 hour

2 large calves' hearts, sliced, tubes and white parts removed

2 tablespoons butter or bacon fat

1 large can tomatoes

2 onions, peeled and chopped

1 large pepper or 2 small peppers, seeded, scraped, and chopped fine

1 cup uncooked rice

1 teaspoon dried basil

salt, pepper

Brown the slices of heart in the butter in a deep skillet or Dutch oven. Add 3 cups of water, cover, and steam until done—perhaps 30 minutes.

Mix the other ingredients together, and put a layer of this mixture in a casserole, then a layer of the slices of heart, and so on until all the ingredients are used. Bake in a 350° oven for 25 to 30 minutes or until the rice is done. Makes 4 servings.

JAN KINDLER'S KIDNEY, MUSHROOM, AND BROWN RICE DISH

Jan Kindler, son of Hans Kindler, conductor of the National Symphony Orchestra for so many years, does his composing in the kitchen.

Time: 20 minutes

2 tablespoons olive oil
½ lb. anise-flavored Italian sausage (removed from casing)
½ lb. fresh mushrooms
½ lb. kidneys—beef, veal or pork preferably—sliced, and white part cut out

1 cup sour cream
½ cup red wine (burgundy, claret, chianti, etc.)
salt
paprika
2 cups hot cooked brown rice

Sauté the sausage in the olive oil, breaking it up with a fork as it browns. Add the mushrooms, brown, and add the sliced kidneys. Cook only 2 or 3 minutes. Add quickly the sour cream, wine, and seasonings. Stir over heat only until warmed—do not cook. (Not more than 5 minutes should elapse from the time the kidneys are put in to serving time.) Mix with the hot cooked rice. Makes 4 servings.

LAMB WITH SPICED GRAPE JAM AND RICE

This is one of the pleasanter ways of finishing up that leg of lamb a few people may have these days. Orange marmalade—the bitter English kind—might be good instead of the jam, but I have never tried it.

Time: 45 minutes if lamb is already cooked; 1½ hours if lamb is uncooked

2 tablespoons fat, preferably bacon drippings
2 to 3 cups diced cooked lamb (or about 1 to 1½ lbs. diced uncooked lamb)

1 jar spiced grape jam or other spicy jam or preserve
1 teaspoon dry English mustard
salt, pepper
3 cups cooked rice

Melt the fat in a skillet and sauté the lamb in it—briefly if the lamb is already cooked; if it is uncooked, brown it, add 2 tablespoons water, cover tightly, and cook over a low flame for about 30 minutes. Next add the jam and mustard, add salt and pepper (more, of course, if the meat is uncooked), and simmer until the jam has melted into a nice pungent sauce. Continue to simmer until the flavors of the meat and sauce are well mingled—about 15 minutes if the meat is cooked, about 35 to 40 minutes if it is uncooked, and in that case add about a cup of water. Pile the rice fluffily on a platter and spoon the lamb-and-jam mixture on top. Makes 4 servings.

ONE MEAT BALL
Iran

In Persia—which is to say Iran—this is not just a phrase from a popular ballad, but a preposterous cooking gesture. Serve the traditional *kuftes* (stuffed meat balls cooked in broth) made into just one large meat ball. Remove from the broth, carve with a flourish, and serve one thick slice to each bowl of broth thickened with lemon and egg. (You may use 8 cups canned beef bouillon instead of the lamb stock.)

Time: 3¼ hours

SOUP

1 lamb bone with a little meat on it
1 onion, sliced
1 clove garlic
1 carrot, sliced
salt, pepper
¼ teaspoon rosemary
2 egg yolks
juice of 1 lemon

MEAT BALL

1 lb. lamb shoulder, ground
1 cup cooked rice
⅓ cup finely chopped fresh parsley
salt, pepper
1 egg, slightly beaten

STUFFING

1 large Bermuda onion (or 2 medium-sized ones), chopped
3 tablespoons butter
3 tablespoons currants
3 tablespoons pine nuts or pignolias
½ teaspoon allspice
½ teaspoon cinnamon

For the soup, simmer the lamb bone, onion, garlic, carrot, salt, pepper, and rosemary in 2 quarts of water for 2 hours; skim off the fat, and strain the broth. Bring to a boil.

Mix the ground lamb with the cooked rice, parsley, salt, pepper, and the slightly beaten egg. Pat into a large ball, smooth and round. For the stuffing, sauté the chopped onion in the butter, remove from the fire, and add the currants, pine nuts, and seasonings. Stir around briefly to mix. Chill for easier handling. Punch a hole in the meat ball, poke the filling in, and pat the hole closed.

Tie the ball in a piece of cheesecloth—or a man's sheer handkerchief—so that all will stay together, and drop into the boiling broth. Cook until the meat ball is done—about 35 to 40 minutes. Remove the ball from the pan, take off the cheesecloth, and put the meat in a warm place. Beat the egg yolks with the lemon juice. Take a spoonful of the broth from the pan, mix with the egg and lemon juice, and add to the soup. Stir until smooth and thickened. Serve in warm soup bowls. Carve the meat ball with grand gestures at the table and serve each person one slice in his bowl of soup. Makes 4 generous servings.

LAMB PILAF
Balkans

A simple recipe for this everyday Balkan dish.

Time: 1½ hours

1½ lbs. lean lamb, cut in small pieces
salt, pepper
3 tablespoons bacon fat
2 medium-sized onions, sliced thin
2½ to 3 cups beef consommé

¾ cup uncooked rice
½ bay leaf
1 hot red pepper, chopped
6 to 8 partly cooked, seeded and quartered prunes
½ lemon, sliced thin

Season the lamb with salt and pepper and sauté in the bacon fat with the sliced onion, cooking gently for 10 minutes. Add 1 cup consommé, cover, and simmer for 20 to 25 minutes. Pour in the rest of the consommé, bring to a boil, and add the rice and the half bay leaf. Add red pepper, meat, onions, lemon, and prunes. Cover and cook in a moderate oven (325°), for 45 minutes. Makes 4 servings.

LAMB PILAF
WITH TOMATO AND RAISINS
Russia

This is a Russian twist to a Balkan dish.

Time: 1 hour

¼ lb. butter
1 lb. lamb shoulder, cut into
  bite-size cubes
2 medium-sized onions,
  chopped
1 cup uncooked rice

2 cups hot beef broth
salt, pepper
1 teaspoon orégano
½ cup scalded seeded raisins
1 teaspoon tomato paste
1 tablespoon melted butter

Sauté the lamb and onions in the butter. Add rice, and stir around until well coated. Pour in the hot broth, add seasonings, cover, and steam until meat and rice are tender—about 30 to 45 minutes. Mix raisins and tomato paste with melted butter, stir into rice and meat, and serve. Makes 4 servings.

AJEM PILAU
Iran

This lamb-and-rice dish is everyday fare in Iran.

Time: 45 minutes

1 lb. lamb shoulder with lots of
  fat, cubed
⅔ cup chopped onion
1 cup uncooked rice
1 teaspoon cinnamon

½ cup fresh chopped tomato,
  or solid-pack canned tomatoes
½ cup pine nuts or pignolias
salt, pepper

Melt the lamb fat in a heavy deep pan and sauté the meat and onions in this until brown. Add the rice, tomato, nuts, and seasoning, and ½ cup of water. Bring to a boil, cover and steam over low heat 20 to 30 minutes or until liquid has evaporated. Makes 4 servings.

HUNGARIAN PORK ROAST

Time: 3 hours, not including soaking time

5 or 6 lbs. rolled and boned shoulder of pork
salt, pepper, flour
½ cup split peas, soaked overnight

2 cups cooked rice
1 medium-sized onion, chopped fine
1 tablespoon celery seed
⅓ cup tomato purée

Rub with salt and pepper and dredge with flour the rolled and boned shoulder of pork. Brown on all sides in a Dutch oven. Add 2½ cups water, cover, and cook in a 350° oven for 2 hours. Cook the split peas in lots of water for 1 hour or until mushy (or cook in pressure cooker according to directions). Drain, mix with the cooked rice, chopped onion, celery seed, and tomato purée. Season with salt and pepper. Pile this mixture around the roast and baste with the juices from the meat. If it seems too dry, add a little boiling water. Cover and cook for 1 hour longer. Makes 4 to 6 servings.

AMERICAN CHOP SUEY

Time: 20 minutes

¼ cup butter or other fat
1 lb. lean pork, cut in thin strips
1 cup chopped onions
2 cups celery, cut in 1-inch strips
2½ cups (No. 2 can) bean sprouts, drained

1½ cups liquid from sprouts plus hot water
1½ teaspoons salt
dash of pepper
2 tablespoons cornstarch
2 teaspoons soy sauce
2 packages (2⅔ cups) pre-cooked rice

Cook rice with 1 teaspoon salt according to directions on package. Meanwhile melt butter in hot skillet. Add meat and brown quickly for 2 minutes. Add onions and sauté for 5 minutes, stirring frequently. Add celery. Drain liquid from canned sprouts and add hot water to make 1½ cups. Add liquid to meat mixture. Add ½ teaspoon salt, and pepper. Cover and boil gently 5 minutes. Add drained bean sprouts, mixing well. Bring to a boil. Blend together 2 tablespoons water, cornstarch, and meat paste, and add to meat. Stir lightly and cook 1 minute. Serve on hot rice. Makes 6 servings.

BAKED HAM SLICE WITH RISOTTO

Serve this prettily arranged on a warm pottery platter, and with a crisp green salad.

Time: 45 minutes

1 slice raw ham, 1 inch thick
1 cup uncooked rice

2 cups chicken broth or bouillon (cubes may be used)

Sauté the slice of ham in its own fat in a heavy skillet that has a lid, browning on both sides. Remove from the pan. Sauté the raw rice in the ham fat until it is well coated. Place the slice of ham on top of the rice and pour in the broth, cover tightly, and bake in a 350° oven about 25 minutes, or until the rice is tender and the liquid all absorbed—or cook more briefly on top of the stove. In desperate cases, water may be substituted for the broth. Makes 4 servings.

EGGPLANT WITH RICE AND HAM

Time: 1 hour

1 medium onion, chopped
1 cup chopped raw ham
3 tablespoons bacon drippings
1 eggplant, peeled and sliced thin
1 cup uncooked rice

1 bay leaf
¼ teaspoon thyme
¼ teaspoon pepper
very little salt
1 cup chicken broth

Fry onion and ham in drippings until onion is pale yellow and ham is browned. Add rice and eggplant and sauté briefly. Add broth and seasoning, cover, and cook 20 to 30 minutes, or until liquid is absorbed and rice is tender. Add more liquid if necessary. Makes 4 to 6 servings.

FRUGAL HAM JAMBALAYA
Louisiana

A simple and everyday version of a Louisiana dish.

Time: 45 minutes

1 onion, chopped or sliced
¼ cup fat
1 No. 2½ can tomatoes
1 cup uncooked rice

1 green pepper, chopped
½ cup ground cooked ham
1 tablespoon curry powder
salt and pepper

Fry onion in fat until golden. Add tomatoes, rice, green pepper, ham, seasoning. Cook until rice has absorbed all the tomato juice— 20 to 30 minutes, adding ¼ cup or more water if the rice starts to dry out before it is tender. Makes 4 servings.

CELERY RICE WITH CREAMED HAM

Time: 15 minutes

1 package (1⅓ cups) pre-
  cooked rice
½ teaspoon salt
1 cup diced celery
1½ cups diced cooked ham
2 tablespoons chopped onion
5 tablespoons butter

¼ cup flour
2½ cups buttermilk
⅛ teaspoon dry mustard
¼ teaspoon Worcestershire
  sauce
1 tablespoon chopped parsley

Cook rice in salted water according to directions on the package.
Meanwhile sauté celery, ham, and onion in 3 tablespoons butter
until light brown. Gradually add flour and blend well. Add buttermilk slowly, stirring constantly. Cook, still stirring, until the mixture
is smooth and thick. Add mustard and Worcestershire sauce. Add
2 tablespoons of butter to the cooked rice. Place rice on a platter,
cover with the creamed ham, and sprinkle with parsley. Makes 4
servings.

ARANCINI DI MOZZARELLA
Italy

This Italian cheese-and-ham fritter is eaten in the Roman *rosticcerias*—one stands around marble counters, munching blissfully. Here serve it with chicken or meat for a main dish, or alone at lunch with a salad. Mozzarella is sold in lumps in all Italian food stores.

Time: 1 hour

1 lump mozzarella, diced
¼ cup diced ham
pinch of orégano
2 tablespoons tomato paste
salt, pepper
2 egg yolks, slightly beaten

½ cup butter, melted
3 cups cooked rice
1 egg, beaten
1 cup breadcrumbs
fat for frying

Mix the mozzarella with the ham, orégano, and tomato paste. Heat until the cheese starts to melt. Remove from fire. Cool. Mix with egg yolks and make into tiny balls. Mix rice with butter. Mold small balls of buttered rice, push smaller balls of the cheese mixture inside, and pat the rice over them. Dip in whole beaten egg and then in breadcrumbs. Fry in deep fat at 375° to 385° until golden brown. Drain on paper towels. Makes 4 servings.

RICE, ONION, AND POTATO CASSEROLE WITH FRESH SAUSAGE
Netherlands

Lusty Dutch fare to serve with beer and a green salad on a cold, bitter day.

Time: 1 hour

1½ lbs. potatoes, peeled and sliced thin (about 4 or 5 medium-sized potatoes)
10 medium-sized onions, chopped coarsely

¾ cup uncooked rice
½ lb. fresh pork sausage
salt
vinegar

Cover the potatoes and onions with water and bring to a boil. Add the well-washed rice and more water if necessary. Bring again to a boil, lower the flame, and simmer for about 30 minutes, or until everything is tender. Meanwhile sauté the sausage in a heavy skillet. When the vegetable mixture is tender, drain it and place in a buttered casserole. Arrange the sausage on top. Bake in a medium oven (350°) for 30 minutes. Sprinkle with vinegar and salt to taste. Makes 6 servings.

5. POULTRY

DANISH CHICKEN

Time: 45 minutes to 1 hour

1 small frying chicken (2 to 2½ lbs.), cut in pieces
2 medium onions, quartered
¼ cup butter or other fat
1¼ teaspoons salt
½ teaspoon paprika
½ teaspoon curry powder
¼ cup catsup
2 tablespoons flour
1 package (1⅓ cups) pre-cooked rice

Sauté chicken and onions in butter until chicken is golden brown. Combine ¾ teaspoon salt, paprika, curry powder, and catsup. Add catsup mixture and 1½ cups hot water to chicken. Cover and simmer 30 minutes, or until tender. Meanwhile cook rice with ½ teaspoon salt, according to directions on the package. When chicken is done, blend flour with ¼ cup water. Add gradually to chicken mixture. Continue cooking, stirring constantly, until sauce is thickened. Arrange chicken and rice on hot platter and pour sauce over all. Makes 4 servings.

CHICKEN BREASTS
WITH GREEN BEANS AND RICE

Time: 1 hour

4 frozen chicken breasts,
thawed, or 2 fresh chicken
breasts, split
butter
1 package frozen green beans
⅔ cup uncooked rice
2 cups chicken broth, or 2
chicken bouillon cubes dissolved in 2 cups water
1 can sliced broiled-in-butter
mushrooms

SAUCE

2 tablespoons butter
2 tablespoons flour
1½ cups milk
2 tablespoons freshly grated
Parmesan cheese
2 tablespoons freshly grated
Swiss cheese
½ teaspoon Worcestershire
sauce
salt, pepper

Roast the chicken breasts in a 350° oven for about 40 minutes, or until they are tender, basting with butter. Cook the beans according to directions on the package. Put rice in a pan with cold chicken broth, bring to a boil, cover, and steam over low heat 14 to 15 minutes, at which time all the liquid should have disappeared, leaving a pan of dry, delicately seasoned, flaky rice.

Meanwhile, make the sauce by melting 2 tablespoons butter and blending with the flour. Add milk slowly and cook until thickened. Add cheese and seasonings. Stir until cheese is melted. Mix green beans and mushrooms with rice, and heat a few minutes if some of the ingredients have cooled. Turn onto deep earthenware platter. Arrange chicken breasts on top and cover with sauce. The dish may be served immediately or prepared ahead and heated for about 20 minutes in a 350° oven. Makes 4 servings.

JIM BEARD'S CHICKEN SMITANE

Jim Beard, author of *The Fireside Cook Book,* says that this is the "only original" version of Guinea Hen Smitane with wild rice, served so expensively in good French restaurants.

Time: 2 hours

1 3-lb. chicken
2 tablespoons butter
1 tablespoon chicken fat or drippings
⅔ cup finely chopped onion

⅓ cup white wine
1 cup sour cream
juice of ½ lemon
3 cups hot cooked rice

Roast the chicken until tender—about 1½ hours in a 350° oven. Save the juices. Cut the chicken in quarters. Melt the butter and chicken fat, and cook the onion in this but do not brown. Add the meat juice and wine to the fat. Let surge and blend. Heat but do not boil. Add lemon juice and sour cream. Place the quarters of chicken on a mound of rice and pour sauce over all. Makes 4 to 6 servings.

ARROZ CON POLLO

This is chicken with rice wherever you see it—Spain, Mexico, West Indies, Latin America, and so on—and there are as many different versions as there are people making it.

Time: 45 minutes to 1¼ hours, depending on age of chicken

2 onions, minced
1 clove garlic
¼ cup olive oil
1 chicken, 3 to 3½ lbs., cut up
   for frying
1 cup uncooked rice

salt, pepper
2 tomatoes, fresh or canned, chopped, or ½ cup tomato juice
pinch of saffron

Sauté the minced onion and the garlic in the olive oil until brown. Discard garlic; remove onion and reserve it. Brown the chicken in the oil. Place chicken and onions in a deep pot. Brown the rice slightly in the same skillet in which onions and chicken were cooked. Add rice to the pot together with the tomatoes (or tomato juice) and salt and pepper. Dissolve a pinch of saffron in hot water and add, together with 1½ cups of water. Cover and simmer slowly until the rice is tender. The rice should have absorbed practically all of the liquid. Cooking time will be approximately 30 minutes; if preferred, the dish can be baked in a 375° oven for 45 minutes. Makes 4 to 6 servings.

PAELLA
Spain

This is Arroz con Pollo with seafood added—mingling its salty flavors with the chicken in a rich, odorous sauce—and a few colorful vegetables strewn about.

Time: 1½ hours

8 good pieces of chicken (breasts and legs—buy separately, or think up what to do with the extra pieces from whole chickens)
flour, salt, pepper
⅓ cup cooking oil, plus more for sprinkling
3 large, fat onions, sliced thick
2 plump cloves garlic, minced
1 large can tomatoes

1 cup uncooked rice, well washed
1 dozen well-scrubbed mussels or clams
1 cup shrimp, cooked and cleaned (or 1 can shrimp)
2 green peppers, seeds scraped out, cut into more or less even strips
⅔ cup cooked fresh peas
2 whole pimientos, cut in strips

Put the pieces of chicken (just one or two at a time) in a paper bag with the flour, salt, and pepper, and shake until lightly coated. Sauté in ⅓ cup oil until brown on all sides; add onions and garlic and cook until they are pale yellow. Add the tomatoes and 1 cup boiling water. Simmer for 30 minutes and then strew the uncooked rice over all and sprinkle oil over that. Cover and simmer 25 to 30 minutes or until rice is tender (it takes a little longer than usual in a thick sauce). Then add the mussels or clams in their shells (the mussels are much the prettiest, but both have a good flavor), and the shrimp. Simmer for about 5 minutes or until the shells are opened. Pour onto a deep warm earthenware platter. Distribute the green pepper, pimiento, and peas decoratively around and serve. Makes 4 to 6 generous servings.

CREOLE CHICKEN

Serve with lots of hot buttered biscuits, and salad, and end up with lime sherbet sprinkled with chocolate chips, and black coffee.

Time: 2 hours

1 5-lb. fowl, cut in serving pieces
3 tablespoons flour
salt, pepper
4 tablespoons chicken fat or butter
½ cup chopped onions
½ clove garlic, minced

2 tablespoons chopped green pepper
3¼ cups (No. 2½ can) tomatoes and juice
¾ cup diced celery
1 small bay leaf
1 package (1⅓ cups) precooked rice

Season the flour with salt and pepper and dredge the pieces of chicken in it, coating lightly. Sauté the chicken in 3 tablespoons of the fat until brown. Add 2 cups water, 2 teaspoons salt, and a dash of pepper. Cover and simmer for 1½ hours, or until chicken is almost tender.

Sauté onions, garlic, and green pepper in remaining tablespoon of fat until vegetables are tender and onion is golden brown. Add to chicken. Break up tomatoes with a fork. Add tomatoes and juice, celery, and bay leaf to chicken. Cover and simmer for 15 minutes. Remove bay leaf. Add rice; mix well. Cover and simmer 15 minutes longer. Makes 4 generous servings.

CHICKEN AND RICE ALEXANDRIA

A rich, bland and elegant dish, suitable for the most impeccable luncheon or Sunday night supper. A tomato aspic and watercress salad goes well with this. Have lots of hot rolls, a dessert if you wish.

Time: ½ hour

1 package (1⅓ cups) pre-cooked rice
4 tablespoons butter
4 tablespoons flour
1 cup chicken broth
1 cup rich milk or 1 cup cream
¼ to ⅓ cup sherry
¼ teaspoon Worcestershire sauce

1 teaspoon salt
dash of pepper
1½ cups diced cooked chicken
1 can (4 oz.) sliced mushrooms
3 tablespoons finely chopped pimientos
2 tablespoons chopped parsley
buttered fine breadcrumbs

Cook rice as directed on package. Melt butter in saucepan; add flour and blend. Add broth and milk gradually, stirring constantly. Cook and stir until mixture is smooth and thickened. Add sherry, Worcestershire sauce, salt, and pepper; blend. Add cooked rice, chicken, mushrooms, pimientos, and parsley. Mix thoroughly.

Pour mixture into a greased 2-quart casserole. Top with buttered crumbs. Bake in hot oven (450°) 10 minutes, or until crumbs are golden brown. Makes 6 servings.

POULET AU RIZ
New Orleans

This recipe comes from Owen Brennan's French and Creole Restaurant in New Orleans, and is a favorite in New Orleans homes, appealing in its simplicity.

Time: 1½ hours

1 whole young chicken, or older one cut in pieces
1 carrot, sliced
1 small onion, sliced
2 stalks celery, chopped
salt, pepper
½ cup uncooked rice
⅓ cup crisp chopped parsley
2 or 3 whole pimientos, chopped coarsely

SAUCE

2 cups broth from the chicken
2 tablespoons chicken fat or butter
2 tablespoons flour
2 egg yolks
2 tablespoons cream

Pick the chicken over carefully, removing any pinfeathers and rinsing inside and out. Put in a deep pot (or Dutch oven) with the carrot, onion, and celery, two quarts of boiling water, and seasoning. Cover and simmer for about 1 hour or until the chicken is tender. Add the rice and simmer about 15 minutes or until the rice is tender. Transfer chicken to warm platter, drain the rice and arrange it around the chicken. Scatter parsley and pimientos here and there. Put in oven to keep warm while making the sauce.

Strain off 2 cups of the broth in which the chicken was cooked, and season it with salt and pepper. Melt the butter or chicken fat, blend in the flour, and, when the mixture has stopped tasting floury, add the broth, stirring constantly while adding. Check seasoning and add more salt and pepper if necessary. Cook until smooth but do not let the sauce thicken too much. Remove from the fire, thicken with egg yolks and cream, and cook briefly until smooth. Pour over the chicken and rice and serve. Makes 4 servings.

CHICKEN-LIVER RISOTTO

No trouble to prepare, the results are wonderful, and the ingredients may be kept on the pantry shelf and in the freezer. Make it on a dreary day when you wish to pamper yourself and/or your guests.

Time: 40 minutes

3 tablespoons olive oil
1 cup uncooked rice
3 cups chicken broth
½ lb. chicken livers

3 tablespoons butter
¼ cup grated Parmesan cheese
salt, pepper

Cook the rice in the olive oil until translucent. Add the chicken broth and cover, and steam until done—about 30 minutes. Meanwhile sauté the chicken livers in butter, then add them to the rice with the grated Parmesan cheese and salt and pepper. Makes 4 servings.

CHICKEN-GIBLET PILAF
WITH PINE NUTS AND RAISINS
Egypt

Chicken giblets at their most impressive. Serve with a peach aspic salad made from the juice of pickled peaches according to the recipe for any basic aspic, and French bread and end the meal with raspberries and sour cream.

Time: 1 hour

⅔ cup chopped chicken giblets
3 cups chicken broth, including that from the giblets
½ cup butter or margarine
¼ cup pine nuts
1 cup uncooked rice

½ cup seedless raisins, washed (soaked in orange juice for a good but most un-Egyptian flavor)
salt, pepper

Simmer the giblets in water until tender—about 30 minutes. Drain, and mix the liquid with the broth. Sauté the pine nuts and rice in the butter until rice is translucent. Add the raisins and giblets. Stir a minute in the butter and then add the chicken broth, salt, and pepper. Bring to a boil, cover, turn heat down. Simmer for about 15 minutes, or until the broth is absorbed and the rice fluffy. Makes 4 servings.

OVEN-BRAISED DUCKLING
WITH WHITE GRAPES

The rice is obligatory with this recipe; potatoes or sweet potatoes would be too heavy. Accompany this with more chilled white wine, and French bread for mopping up gravy. A blueberry tart with a marmalade glaze would make a fine finale—and, naturally, coffee.

Time: 1¾ hours

1 5- to 6-lb. Long Island duckling, dressed weight
1 tablespoon duck fat
¼ cup finely diced onion
1 teaspoon salt
⅛ teaspoon pepper
1 cup white wine, or duck broth

1 package (1⅓ cups) pre-
cooked rice
1 tablespoon cornstarch
½ teaspoon Kitchen Bouquet
1 cup halved white grapes, seedless or seeded

Prepare duck as for roasting, cutting off wing tips and neck. Cut duck in quarters, cutting out backbone. Place duck, skin side up, on rack in shallow roasting pan. Roast in slow oven, 325°, for 1 hour. Meanwhile cook giblets, neck, backbone and wing tips in 2 cups boiling salted water until tender, about 45 minutes. Strain off broth. Allow fat to rise and pour it off. Heat 1 tablespoon fat in small pan and add onion. Let cook about 3 minutes. Add seasonings and broth or wine. Bring to boil. Transfer quartered duck to deep pan. Pour broth and onion over duck. Cover tightly and bake at 325° until duck is tender—about 30 minutes longer. Meanwhile, cook rice according to directions on the package. When ready to serve, remove duck to warm serving platter. Blend together corn-starch, 1 tablespoon cold water, and Kitchen Bouquet and add to broth in baking pan, stirring over low heat until sauce thickens. Add grapes to sauce and pour over duck. Pile rice decoratively around duck on platter. Makes 4 generous servings.

ROAST SQUAB
WITH WILD RICE STUFFING
AND BAKED FRUIT

This is a meal to end all meals—pay the budget no mind. And while you're in that mood, serve satiny heads of Belgian endive (the pale, bitter kind) with a bland French dressing—four parts olive oil, one part lemon juice, dash of grated lemon peel, salt, and freshly ground black pepper—and lots of crusty French bread. Meringues with strawberries soaked in Kirsch, slightly sweetened whipped cream, and black coffee should follow.

Time: 1¾ hours

⅔ cup uncooked wild rice, well washed
3 cups chicken bouillon (or 3 cubes dissolved in 3 cups of water)
salt
3 tablespoons butter
2 tablespoons finely chopped onion
4 squabs, cleaned and picked over

½ lemon
¼ cup melted butter

1 No. 1 can apricot halves, with juice
1 8-oz. can seedless grapes or 1 cup fresh white seedless grapes
1 6-oz. package of salted almonds, slivered (nice, but not obligatory)

Simmer the wild rice, covered, in the chicken broth until it is tender and the liquid has been absorbed. This will take about 45 minutes. Salt lightly. Sauté the onions in butter briefly until pale yellow but not mushy, and mix with rice. Rub the squabs inside and out with the half-lemon and sprinkle with salt. Fill with wild rice, being careful not to pack them too tightly. Roast uncovered in a 325° oven for 45 minutes or until tender, basting from time to time with melted butter.

Fill the apricot halves with white grapes and almonds. Put about ½ cup of the apricot juice in the bottom of a shallow casserole, and add the stuffed halves. When the squabs have been baking for 35 minutes, put the apricot casserole in the oven and bake until the squabs are done. Serve together. Makes 4 servings.

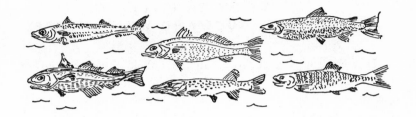

6. SEAFOOD

BAKED FISH
WITH RICE-AND-EGG STUFFING
Russia

Serve this impressively on a ceramic fish platter, or on a wooden plank. It should be accompanied by a tomato, cucumber, and chicory salad, well coated with a classic French dressing. Heat brown-and-serve salt sticks to go with this, and end up with cheesecake and coffee.

Time: 55 minutes

1 4-lb. fish (haddock or bass)
2 cups cooked rice
6 fillets of anchovy, cut in pieces
4 hard-cooked eggs, chopped

¼ teaspoon chopped parsley
2 egg yolks
salt, pepper
breadcrumbs
6 tablespoons butter

Mix rice, anchovy, hard-cooked eggs, parsley, pepper, butter, and raw egg yolks. Rub the inside of the fish with salt. Fill with rice and egg stuffing. Skewer closed. Rub with breadcrumbs. Melt butter, pour over fish, and add 2 tablespoons water. Bake in 350° oven for 45 minutes, basting with the juices in the pan from time to time. Makes 4 to 6 generous servings.

BETTY'S FISH FILLETS
WITH CHEESE SAUCE AND WHITE GRAPES
England

This English dish disproves all the unkind things people say about English food. Peel and seed the white grapes in front of your guests—they'll be no end impressed and amused. The day you're in no mood for this, use an 8-oz. can of seeded grapes. The grapes are a necessary accent in an otherwise bland dish.

Time: 45 minutes

1 cup uncooked rice	**CHEESE SAUCE**
2 cups chicken broth	2 tablespoons butter
1 stick of butter (¼ lb.)	2 tablespoons flour
1 lb. fillets of fresh or frozen fish	1 cup chicken broth
(any delicately flavored kind)	⅔ cup grated Cheddar cheese
⅓ lb. white grapes, peeled and	½ cup cream
seeded, or 1 8-oz. can white	salt
grapes, drained	paprika

Put the rice in 2 cups chicken broth, bring to fast rolling boil, cover and steam over low flame for 15 minutes without peeking.

Meanwhile make the sauce. Melt the butter and add the flour. Blend, add 1 cup chicken broth, and cook until smooth. Add cheese and stir until cheese is melted. Add cream and seasoning and heat over low flame, stirring occasionally.

Put the cooked rice in the bottom of a casserole or deep earthenware platter. Roll each fish fillet around a lump of butter the size of a walnut, and arrange on the top of the rice. (If frozen fillets are not thawed completely, arrange them in serving-size chunks with lumps of butter between them on top of the rice.) Cover with the cheese sauce, sprinkle the white grapes on top, and bake in a 350° oven for about 15 minutes. Makes 4 servings.

FISH PIE
Russia

Whether baked in a loaf or pie pan, this concoction of dough, fish, rice, and various accompaniments is just another form of Italian pizza—or, for that matter, any pie used as a main dish.

Time: 45 minutes

¼ lb. fresh mushrooms
3 tablespoons butter
yeast dough or pie dough
  (double crust) to fit 9-inch
  pan

2 cups rice cooked in bouillon
1 lb. cooked or smoked fish, cut
  in small pieces
salt, pepper
1 pint sour cream

Sauté the mushrooms in butter. Line a pie pan with the dough. Spread on this a layer of rice, and a layer each of fish, mushrooms, salt, pepper, and sour cream. Repeat until all ingredients are used. Cover with top crust and pinch closed. Bake in hot (450°) oven until dough is done—15 to 25 minutes. Makes 4 servings.

OYSTER JAMBALAYA

Time: 25 minutes

2 small green peppers, sliced
1 pint oysters and their liquor
2 cups cooked rice
2 slices chopped cooked bacon

1 onion, minced
salt and pepper
breadcrumbs
butter

Simmer peppers in small amount of water until barely tender. Add oysters and liquor and cook just until the edges begin to curl. Mix with bacon, onion, and rice. Season and transfer to a buttered casserole. Cover with breadcrumbs, dot with butter, and bake at 350° for 15 minutes. Makes 4 servings.

RICE RING WITH SEAFOOD SAUCE

Time: 45 minutes

3 tablespoons butter
3 tablespoons flour
1½ cups chicken broth or
   bouillon
3 tablespoons brandy
salt
cayenne
freshly grated nutmeg
1 can smoked oysters or mussels

1 can crabmeat or lobster, in
   chunks, with thin bony parti-
   tions removed
1 lb. cooked, cleaned, and
   peeled shrimp—fresh, frozen,
   or canned
1 Buttered Rice Ring (see
   index), pint-size or larger

Melt butter and blend in the flour. Add chicken broth, stirring constantly, until sauce is smooth and thick. Add brandy, salt, cayenne, and dash of freshly grated nutmeg. Add the seafood and heat briefly. Heat rice ring and unmold onto a warm platter, and fill center with the seafood sauce. Makes 4 servings.

CRAB RISOTTO

Time: 45 minutes

1 cup uncooked rice
2 medium-sized onions,
   chopped
3 tablespoons olive oil
2 8-oz. cans tomato sauce
⅓ cup chopped parsley

1 clove garlic
¾ lb. fresh crabmeat or 2
   6½-oz. cans crabmeat,
   picked over and membranes
   removed
grated Parmesan cheese

Cook the rice with the onions in the olive oil until the rice is translucent and the onion pale yellow. Add the tomato sauce, cover, and steam until done. Add the parsley, garlic, crabmeat, and grated Parmesan cheese. Cook over a very low flame until all the ingredients are hot and the cheese has melted into them. Makes 4 servings.

LOBSTER OR SHRIMP RING WITH CHEESE SAUCE

Time: ½ hour

2 tablespoons butter
1 medium-sized onion, chopped
3 cups hot cooked rice
1 large (No. 2½) can tomatoes
1 bay leaf
1 tablespoon capers
2 cups diced cooked lobster or shrimp

SAUCE

3 tablespoons butter
3 tablespoons flour
1½ cups milk
1 teaspoon dry mustard
salt
paprika
½ cup grated sharp cheese

Sauté the onion in butter and add to the cooked rice. Cook the tomatoes with the bay leaf until they are thickened. Add to the rice with the lobster or shrimp, and capers. Butter a ring mold and fill with rice, tomato, and shellfish mixture. Heat briefly in the oven. Meanwhile make sauce by melting the butter and blending in the flour. Cook several minutes, then add the milk gradually, stirring constantly until smooth and thickened. Add seasoning and cheese and stir until cheese is melted. Unmold the rice ring and fill the center with cheese sauce. Makes 4 to 6 servings.

SHRIMP-AND-OYSTER JAMBALAYA
New Orleans

This is the traditional dish as served at Owen Brennan's French and Creole Restaurant in New Orleans. Like other notable and savory mishmashes, it may be varied according to the inclinations of individual cooks and the supplies in their larders. Serve with lots of French bread and a crisp tossed green salad.

Time: 1 hour

1 tablespoon butter
1 tablespoon flour
1 medium onion, chopped fine
1 medium-thick slice cooked ham, chopped fine
3 ripe tomatoes, peeled and chopped

½ lb. raw shrimp, peeled and de-veined
1 hot red pepper pod, cut in pieces and seeds scraped out
salt
¾ cup uncooked rice
1 dozen oysters and their liquor

Melt the butter, add flour, and cook over a low flame until smooth and brown. Add onion and ham, stirring constantly to keep from burning. Add the tomatoes, shrimp, pepper pod, salt, 1 cup water, and the rice. Bring to a boil, cover, and turn flame very low. Cook together until rice is done—which is when the moisture is absorbed and the rice tender but not mushy. Add the oysters and their liquor and cook until their edges just begin to curl. Serve immediately. Makes 4 servings.

CHINESE SHRIMP AND BEANS

A Chinese dish adapted to American ways.

Time: ½ hour

1 package frozen shrimp or ¾ lb. fresh shrimp, cooked, peeled, and cleaned
½ teaspoon grated onion
4 tablespoons fat
1 cup chicken bouillon or 1 chicken bouillon cube dissolved in 1 cup boiling water

¾ teaspoon salt
⅛ teaspoon pepper
1 tablespoon cornstarch
1 package frozen green beans, French style, or ¾ to 1 lb. fresh green beans
1 package (1⅓ cups) precooked rice

Dice the shrimp or leave them whole, as desired. Sauté the shrimp with onion in the fat until shrimp are lightly browned. Add ¼ teaspoon salt, pepper, and bouillon; bring to a boil. Blend cornstarch with ¼ cup cold water and add to shrimp mixture. Cook and stir until slightly thickened. Keep hot. Cook frozen beans as directed on package, reducing cooking time to 5 minutes. (If fresh beans are used, prepare, and cook 10 to 15 minutes.) Drain; add to shrimp mixture. Cook rice with ½ teaspoon salt according to directions on the package. Arrange rice on serving dish and cover with shrimp mixture. Serve with soy sauce. Makes 4 servings.

SHRIMP CREOLE

Louisiana people serve Shrimp Creole in as many versions, and as often, as other people do stew—naturally, with lots of French or garlic bread to sop up the juices, and a crisp, tossed salad.

Time: 40 minutes

1 box frozen shrimp or ¾ lb. fresh shrimp, cooked, peeled, and cleaned
¼ cup diced green pepper
¼ cup minced onion
½ cup diced celery
3 tablespoons butter or other fat
1 tablespoon flour
1⅓ cups canned tomatoes

1 teaspoon salt
dash of pepper
1 teaspoon sugar
1 bay leaf
1 tablespoon chopped parsley
½ teaspoon Worcestershire sauce
1 package (1⅓ cups) precooked rice

Sauté green pepper, onion, and celery in butter for 5 minutes. Add flour and blend. Add tomatoes gradually, stirring constantly. Add ½ teaspoon salt, pepper, sugar, bay leaf, and parsley, and cook gently 30 minutes. Remove bay leaf and parsley. Add shrimp and Worcestershire sauce. Meanwhile, cook rice according to directions on the package, with ½ teaspoon salt. Arrange on platter. Cover with shrimp mixture. Serve at once. Makes 4 generous servings.

SHRIMP MULL

This recipe is another piece of Southern Americana.

Time: 2 hours

¼ cup chopped onion
1 clove garlic, sliced
3 tablespoons melted butter
2¼ cups (No. 2 can) canned tomatoes
½ cup catsup
½ teaspoon celery seed
dash of Tabasco sauce
¼ teaspoon Worcestershire sauce

2 teaspoons salt
⅛ teaspoon pepper
1 teaspoon lemon juice
1 lb. raw shrimp, peeled and de-veined, or 1 box frozen shrimp
¼ cup fine cracker crumbs
1 package (1⅓ cups) pre-cooked rice

Put onion and garlic in saucepan with butter. Cook until onion is tender. Add tomatoes, 2 cups water, catsup, Tabasco sauce, celery seed, pepper, and 1½ teaspoons salt. Cover and simmer 1 to 2 hours (the longer it cooks, the better the flavor). Add lemon juice and shrimp and cook 5 minutes. Add cracker crumbs. Bring mixture to a boil, stirring constantly. Cook the precooked rice with ½ teaspoon salt according to directions on the package. Serve shrimp over rice. Makes 4 servings.

SHRIMP
IN SOUR CREAM AND WINE SAUCE

Time: ½ hour

1 cup white wine
2 cups sour cream
1 teaspoon thyme
salt
2 lbs. large fresh shrimp,
cooked, peeled, and cleaned

1 cup rice cooked in chicken
broth
1 tablespoon butter or chicken
fat

Mix the wine with the sour cream, thyme, and salt, until smooth and creamy. Add the shrimp. Spread the rice on the bottom of a buttered casserole and pour the shrimp sauce over it. Dot with butter or chicken fat. Bake in a 350° oven for about 20 minutes or just until hot and the flavors well mingled. Makes 4 servings.

SHRIMP PILAU
Charleston

Time: 1¼ hours

4 slices bacon
1 small onion, minced
2½ cups canned tomatoes

1 cup uncooked rice
¾ lb. fresh shrimp, cooked and
cleaned

Mince the bacon and fry until crisp. Drain on paper towels. Sauté onion in bacon fat. Add tomatoes and, when they are hot, add rice. Cook over very low flame until rice is cooked—about 40 minutes. Mix in bacon and shrimp, and turn into buttered casserole. Bake at 350° for 15 minutes. Makes 4 to 6 servings.

CLAMS OR MUSSELS
STEAMED IN THEIR SHELLS WITH RICE

This dish, gusty with garlic and the good smell of the sea, is only for those who take their shellfish and garlic seriously and reverently. Serve in large warm soup bowls, accompanied by French bread and a crisp green salad.

Time: 25 minutes

½ cup olive oil
3 cloves garlic
4 large onions, chopped
1 bunch parsley, minced
1½ cups uncooked rice

salt and freshly ground black pepper
24 large or 32 small clams, or 36 mussels, shells well scrubbed

Cook the garlic, onions, and parsley in olive oil until the onions are pale yellow but *not* until they lose their crispness. Add the rice and 2 cups of water and seasoning. Bring to a boil. Cover and turn heat low. Cook for 12 minutes. Then add the clams or mussels still in their shells (their juices will add the rest of the needed liquid). Cover and steam for 3 to 5 minutes. Makes 4 generous servings.

MUSSEL OR CLAM PILAF

This is a delicate and yet filling dish, unusual and yet not time-consuming to make.

Time: ½ hour

3 strips bacon, cut into pieces
1 medium-sized onion and 1 small onion, chopped (keep them separate)
3 medium-sized tomatoes, peeled, seeded, and chopped
2 cups bouillon
1 teaspoon salt

1 teaspoon sugar
pinch of pepper
1 tablespoon brandy
3 cups hot cooked rice
½ cup dry white wine
1½ lbs. mussels or clams, shells well scrubbed
2 tablespoons chopped parsley

Sauté the bacon over low heat until partly crisp. Remove, drain on a paper towel. Pour off surplus drippings, leaving just enough in the pan barely to cover the bottom. Sauté the medium-sized onion in this until pale yellow. Add the chopped tomatoes and sauté them very briefly, then add the bouillon, sugar, salt, pepper, and brandy. Simmer until thick. Put the wine and small onion in a pan with the mussels or clams. Cover and steam just until the shells open. Remove the shellfish from the pan. Strain the wine and juices into the sauce. Mound the rice on a warm platter and arrange the shellfish symmetrically on the rice. Pour the sauce over the rice, sprinkle with parsley and bacon, and serve immediately. Makes 4 servings.

STUFFED MUSSELS (MEDIA DOLMA)
Armenia

A simpler, less costly, and spicier Armenian version of a New Orleans oyster dish. Serve either as a main dish or as hors d'oeuvre.

Time: 1¼ hours

⅓ cup olive oil
4 onions, chopped
½ cup uncooked rice, well washed
1 teaspoon allspice

salt, pepper
¼ cup pine nuts
4 teaspoons dried currants
2 dozen mussels

Heat the oil, and cook the onion in it till golden. Add rice, 1 teaspoon allspice, salt and pepper, and cool. Mix with pine nuts and currants. Scrub mussels until the shells are clear and gleaming. Put in cold water. Cover and steam over a low flame just until shells are open and flesh is pale orange—about 2 to 5 minutes. Drain mussels, saving liquid. Remove beard and take off top shell. Press rice-and-onion stuffing over the meat in each shell. Put in a greased casserole. Pour 2 cups liquid (mussel liquor and water) over them. Cover and bake in 325° oven for 45 minutes, or over low heat until the water evaporates. Makes 4 generous servings.

7. FRUGAL AND FILLING MAIN DISHES

NEW ORLEANS RED BEANS AND RICE

This recipe from Ella Brennan, who works with her brother, Owen, in his French and Creole restaurant in New Orleans, is so enchanting in its unstereotyped style that it is given here "as is." Here's how to prepare the beans and use them with the boiled rice in that most typical of Southern recipes—truly a New Orleans dish —Red Beans and Rice.

Time: 2½ to 3 hours

Take approximately 2 cups of red beans, wash, and pick out the dry or broken beans. Soak in warm water for an hour. Wash and drain. Put on fire with sufficient water to cover the beans and commence them to boiling. Add 2 medium-sized onions, chopped fine, salt, and add the oleo or butter to richen up. Boil the beans until they mash tender. Some folks like them soupy, others a little thick. If you don't want them with a rather thin gravy, thicken with a little bit of flour, but this is not the best preferred fashion. If meat is desired, add sweet pickled pork soon enough that it will be boiled tender while the beans are boiling. If the pickled pork is used, be careful not to salt the beans additionally, since they will absorb some of the salt from the meat. When the beans are creamy soft, dish up and spread over the rice, steaming hot.

Makes 6 generous servings.

RED BEANS AND RICE

When times are good, small pieces of ham or salt pork may be
added to this mélange. In Tampa black beans are cooked with the
rice. In Nassau and the West Indies dried peas are often used.

Time: ½ hour

½ cup chopped onions
2 tablespoons butter or other
  fat
1 package (1⅓ cups) pre-
  cooked rice
1 teaspoon salt

⅛ teaspoon pepper
2 cups tomato juice and liquid
  from red beans
2 cups (No. 2 can) red kidney
  beans, drained
½ cup grated sharp cheese

Sauté onions in the butter in saucepan until onions are tender.
Add precooked rice, salt, pepper, and tomato juice and bean liquid.
Bring to a full rolling boil. Remove from heat. Cover and let stand
10 minutes. Add beans and reheat. Serve at once, topped with
grated cheese. Makes 4 to 6 servings.

This may be made with plain water instead of tomato juice, or
with a tablespoon of lemon juice or vinegar added to the tomato
juice.

CHINESE FRIED RICE

This is one of the amiable dishes that never bore by being the same. Use any this-and-that in the refrigerator, just so there are pleasing contrasts in flavor, color, and texture. For instance, mushrooms, bean sprouts, bits of cooked pork, green ginger, and so on may be used as variations.

Time: 20 minutes

3 tablespoons oil, preferably peanut oil
2 large onions, chopped (or 3 or 4 spring onions, tops and bottoms chopped)
3 or 4 stalks celery, cut in 1-inch pieces

2 cups cooked rice
1 cup cleaned and cooked shrimp
½ cup sliced water chestnuts
¼ cup soy sauce

Sauté the onions and celery in the oil until pale yellow. Add the rice, shrimp, water chestnuts, and soy sauce. Stir until thoroughly mixed, cover, and simmer for about 10 minutes, or until really hot. Serve immediately. Makes 4 servings.

ITALIAN BAKED RICE

This can be a meal in itself when served with an ample salad and lots of hot biscuits, and followed with a fruit and cheese dessert.

Time: 40 minutes

1 medium-sized onion, chopped
¼ cup butter
½ lb. Italian sausage, skinned and chopped fine
1 small (8-oz.) can hearts of artichokes, drained and sliced thin

½ package frozen peas, or 1 cup raw fresh peas
3 tablespoons diced mushrooms
¾ cup meat stock
3 cups cooked rice
⅓ cup grated Parmesan cheese

Sauté the onion and sausage in the butter until a light brown. Add peas and artichoke slices and brown these. Add mushrooms. Pour in ¼ cup of the meat stock and simmer for about 10 minutes. Add the rice and turn the mixture into a greased casserole. Add the rest of the stock and sprinkle the top with the Parmesan cheese. Bake in a hot (375°) oven until the cheese is a brown, bubbly crust —about 15 to 20 minutes. Makes 4 servings.

KEDGEREE
India

This lentil-and-rice combination can accompany almost any dish from meat with curry sauce to just plain roast or broiled meat. Egyptian lentils are much the prettiest—a rosy orange, turning yellow as they cook. If none are available to you locally, they may be ordered from the Atlas Importing Company, 1109 Second Avenue, New York.

Time: 2 hours, not including soaking time

1 cup lentils (preferably Egyptian lentils), soaked for at least 1 hour
7 or 8 peppercorns
7 or 8 cardamon seeds (the black ones inside small white pods)

1 bay leaf
1 piece green ginger
salt
1 large onion, sliced thin
2 tablespoons oil
1 cup uncooked rice

Put the lentils in 3 quarts of water. Add the seasonings, tied in a piece of cheesecloth. Bring to a boil and simmer about 1½ hours or until lentils become tender and, if Egyptian, turn yellow (other lentils stay the same color). Sauté the onion in the oil, add to the lentils with the rice, and cook until liquid is absorbed and rice is tender. Remove the bag of seasonings and serve. Makes 4 to 6 servings.

JAGASEE
New England

A Down-East legume-and-rice concoction, especially good for the young and hearty who are almost impossible to fill up. Serve with lots of hot cornbread and a salad with tomatoes, pieces of raw cauliflower, celery, green pepper, and so on.

Time: 12 hours

2 cups dried lima beans
2 large Bermuda onions, sliced
2 tablespoons fat, preferably bacon fat
½ lb. salt pork, cubed and scalded
1 large (No. 2½) can tomatoes

⅔ cup diced green pepper, seeds removed
⅔ cup diced celery, leaves and stalks
2 cups uncooked rice
salt, pepper

Soak the lima beans overnight, then simmer until skins curl back when blown upon—about 1 hour. Sauté the onions in the fat until pale yellow. Transfer to a casserole with a tightly fitting top. Add the cooked beans, the scalded pork, the tomatoes, green pepper, celery, rice, and seasoning. Cover tightly and bake in a medium oven (350°) for about 3 hours, adding some water when the dish starts to dry out. Makes 6 to 8 generous servings.

HOPPING JOHN
South Carolina

Green beans and pot likker and Hopping John creep into all Southern speeches when the speaker gets emotional and nostalgic.

Time: 10½ hours

2 cups cow peas, soaked overnight
¼ lb. salt pork or other seasoning meat

1 cup uncooked rice
3 tablespoons bacon drippings

Boil the peas with salt pork until tender—1½ to 2 hours, or 30 minutes in a pressure cooker. Add the peas and 3 cups of the water in which they were cooked to rice and drippings. Cook over slow fire for one hour. Makes 6 servings.

BAKED EGGS WITH RICE

The rounded humps of the eggs make a pleasing pattern in the dish.

Time: 25 minutes

2 tablespoons butter
2 tablespoons flour
1 tablespoon curry powder
salt, paprika
½ small onion, minced

2 cups milk
6 hard-cooked eggs
1½ cups cooked rice
bread or cracker crumbs

Blend the butter and flour over low heat and cook for a minute; then add the curry powder, salt, paprika, and onion. Cook for a minute longer. Gradually add milk, stirring constantly until the sauce is smooth and thickened. Butter a shallow oval or round baking dish and make a border of the rice. Cut eggs in half lengthwise and arrange in the center of the dish, cut side down. Pour sauce over all, covering rice and eggs. Sprinkle with fine bread or cracker crumbs, dot with butter, and bake in a 350° oven about 20 minutes or until nicely browned. Makes 2 to 3 servings.

EGG PILAU
South Carolina

A Charleston lunch or supper dish, this is also a good thing to keep in mind for Lent.

Time: ½ hour

1 cup uncooked rice
2 cups chicken broth or bouillon
salt

paprika
4 eggs
½ cup butter
⅓ cup finely chopped parsley

Put rice in saucepan with the chicken broth, salt, and paprika. Bring to a boil, cover, and simmer over low heat 20 minutes or until rice is tender and liquid all absorbed. Break the eggs into a bowl, then slide them into the rice. Add parsley and butter. Remove from heat and stir for a couple of minutes. The heat of the rice will cook the eggs and melt the butter. Makes 4 servings.

BAKED ONIONS
STUFFED WITH WILD RICE

This recipe presumes that you have such a thing as cold cooked wild rice lying around in the refrigerator.

Time: 1½ hours

8 medium-sized or 4 large Bermuda onions
½ cup grated Parmesan or
   Swiss cheese

1 cup cooked wild rice
salt, pepper
½ cup milk

Boil the onions until tender, and save about ½ cup of the juice. Carefully scoop out the centers of the onions, leaving about a ½-inch shell. Mix the rice with the cheese and seasoning and pile in the cavities. Dribble some of the milk into each one. Put in a baking dish. Pour the onion juice in the bottom and bake in a medium oven for about 15 to 20 minutes, or until the cheese is brown and bubbly. Serve in the dish. Makes 4 servings.

STUFFED GRAPE LEAVES
Greece

Either buy canned grape leaves in a Greek delicatessen, or drop fresh ones (12 or more large ones for this amount of rice) into boiling water for a minute or two to make them pliable. Drain and use as directed. These may be served as the main dish in almost any type of meal—American or Balkan.

Time: 1¼ hours

2 medium-sized onions, chopped fine
¼ cup olive oil
1 cup uncooked rice
⅓ cup pine nuts
1 tablespoon chopped parsley or mint
½ teaspoon allspice
juice of ½ lemon
salt, pepper
1 can grape leaves, well drained, or 12 fresh leaves

Brown the onions in the oil. Add the rice, pine nuts, parsley, lemon juice, allspice, salt, and pepper. Add 1 cup warm water and cook until liquid is absorbed. Put a spoonful of the mixture on each leaf. Roll up and secure with a toothpick. Put the plump rolls in a casserole with 1 cup water. Cover and bake in a medium oven (350°) for 45 minutes or until liquid is absorbed. Makes 4 servings.

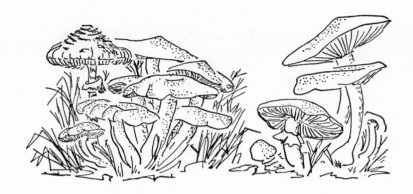

8. SIDE DISHES

RICE WITH MUSHROOMS

This dish goes best with ham or roast chicken.

Time: 15 minutes

3 tablespoons butter, or more
½ small onion, chopped
4 tablespoons flour
salt
1 cup meat stock or beef bouillon

½ lb. fresh mushrooms, sliced
Japanese fashion, lengthwise
through the caps and stems
2 cups hot cooked rice

Sauté onion in 2 tablespoons butter until brown and then remove onion. Add flour and salt to butter, and cook until brown, stirring all the while. Add meat stock or bouillon gradually and cook for about 2 minutes, stirring constantly. Sauté the mushrooms in 1 tablespoon or more of butter, and add them and the onions to the sauce. Pour over a mound of hot fluffy rice. Makes 4 servings.

PARCHED RICE
WITH TOMATO SAUCE AND CHEESE

Serve with ham or tongue (hot or cold) or pork, a bitter green salad with a sharp French dressing, and hot cornbread.

Time: 40 minutes

1 cup uncooked rice
1 large onion, chopped
2 tablespoons butter
1 to 1½ cups bouillon or beef broth
1 large (No. 2½ can) tomatoes
½ can Italian tomato paste
1 teaspoon Worcestershire sauce
1 teaspoon English mustard
salt
1 cup diced Swiss cheese or American Cheddar cheese

Spread the raw rice in a large, dry, heavy skillet. Put over low heat and shake or stir constantly until the rice is a beautiful toast color. Sauté the onion briefly in butter, and add onion and butter to the parched rice. Pour in 1 cup bouillon, tomatoes (juice and all), and tomato paste and seasonings. Stir and bring to a fast boil, then cover tightly and simmer over low heat for 20 minutes. Stir the diced cheese into the rice mixture. Cover and steam until rice is tender and cheese partly melted, which should be about 5 to 10 minutes more. Add ½ cup bouillon or water if rice starts to dry out before tender. When done, all the liquid should be absorbed. Makes 4 generous servings.

RIZ AU GRATIN
France

A French accompaniment to an important piece of meat. Serve with a green vegetable, tossed salad, and hunks of French bread. Put a period to the meal with fresh fruit.

Time: 40 minutes

2 tablespoons butter	½ cup grated Swiss cheese
2 tablespoons flour	salt
2 cups milk	breadcrumbs
3 cups boiled rice	grated Parmesan cheese

Make a white sauce by melting the butter, stirring in the flour until well blended, then gradually adding the milk and cooking until thick. Add the rice and the grated Swiss cheese and salt. Turn into a buttered casserole, sprinkle with breadcrumbs, and dot with bits of butter. Then sprinkle à bit of grated Parmesan cheese over top and bake in a hot oven for 15 to 20 minutes, or until brown and bubbly. Makes 4 to 6 servings.

MEXICAN FRIED RICE

Time: 45 minutes

1 cup uncooked rice
4 tablespoons butter or oil
2 tomatoes, chopped, or 1 cup
   tomato juice
2 onions, chopped

4 cloves garlic
1 teaspoon salt
2 cups hot broth or bouillon
   (any kind) or water

Wash rice in 3 waters and drain. Melt butter or heat oil in a large skillet that has a tightly fitting lid, add the rice, and stir until each grain is coated with fat. Cook over low flame until the rice begins to brown. Add the tomatoes or juice, the chopped onions, garlic, salt, and broth (or water, but water is just water), and bring to a boil. Put lid on skillet, turn flame as low as possible, and cook until all of the liquid has been absorbed—about ½ hour. Do not stir while the rice is cooking. Makes 4 servings.

TOMATO PILAF

Time: 45 minutes

¼ cup butter
1 cup uncooked rice
1 cup chicken or beef broth
1 cup tomato juice

2 fresh tomatoes, skinned and
   chopped
salt, pepper

Melt butter in heavy skillet and add dry rice. Stir until the grains are well coated and the mixture bubbly. Bring to a boil tomato juice mixed with chicken or beef broth. Pour over the rice. Add tomatoes, salt, pepper. Cover and cook slowly in the oven or on top of the stove for about 30 minutes. Makes 4 servings.

TOMATO RICE

This is especially good with broiled or fried fish or shrimp.

Time: 45 minutes

4 slices bacon, cut in pieces
1 large onion or 2 medium-sized onions, chopped
1 large (No. 2½ can) tomatoes
2 tablespoons sugar

salt, pepper
½ cup sour cream or evaporated milk
3 cups hot cooked rice

Fry the bacon until crisp. Remove the bacon and keep warm. Cook the onions in the bacon fat until pale yellow, then add the tomatoes, sugar, salt, and pepper. Cook until smooth and thick. Meanwhile heat the sour cream slightly (cooking will curdle it and detract from its appearance, though its taste will not change). Remove the tomato mixture from the stove and add the sour cream and mix. Pour over the rice, sprinkle with bits of bacon, and serve. Makes 4 servings.

BROCCOLI RICE SOUFFLÉ

This may be served with mushroom, egg, or cheese sauce. It is a good accompaniment to ham.

Time: 1½ hours

½ package (⅔ cup) pre-cooked rice
1¼ teaspoons salt
1 box frozen chopped broccoli, or 1½ cups finely chopped cooked fresh broccoli
3 tablespoons butter
3 tablespoons flour

1½ cups milk
dash of cayenne
dash of pepper
3 eggs, separated; yolks beaten until thick and lemon-colored, whites until stiff
1 teaspoon grated onion

Combine rice, ¾ cup water, and ¼ teaspoon salt in saucepan, and cook according to directions on the package. Cook broccoli, drain, and chop very fine. Melt butter in a saucepan. Add flour, blending well. Add milk gradually, stirring constantly. Then add 1 teaspoon salt, cayenne, and pepper, and cook and stir over low heat until thickened. Add hot mixture to egg yolks and mix well. Stir in onion, broccoli, and rice. Add very gradually to egg whites, folding in thoroughly. Pour mixture into greased 1½-quart casserole. Place in pan of hot water and bake in slow oven (325°) 1 hour, or until soufflé is firm. Makes 5 or 6 servings.

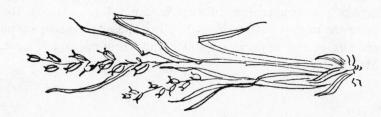

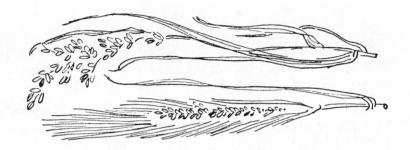

BROCCOLI CASSEROLE
WITH FANCY TOPPING

This tastes better than it sounds on first reading.

Time: 35 minutes

1 package (1⅓ cups) pre-
  cooked rice
1 teaspoon salt
3 tablespoons slivered blanched
  almonds
3 tablespoons butter

2 cups chopped cooked broccoli
  or asparagus
2 tomatoes, sliced
pepper
1 egg white
¾ cup mayonnaise

Combine rice, 1½ cups water, and ½ teaspoon salt in a saucepan, and cook according to directions on the package. Sauté almonds in butter until golden brown. Add to rice; blend. Add broccoli or asparagus; mix well. Turn into greased 1½-quart casserole. Arrange sliced tomatoes over top. Season tomatoes with salt and pepper and brush with butter. Place casserole under broiler 8 to 10 minutes, or until tomatoes are lightly browned.

Meanwhile, beat egg white until it will stand in soft peaks. Add mayonnaise and blend well. Spread over tomatoes and return casserole to broiler for 2 minutes or until topping is golden brown. Makes 6 servings.

RISI PISI

Austria and Hungary

This can be an infinitely varied dish—just so there are rice and fresh peas. From then on, you may add what you will—onion, parsley, bacon, and so on. Serve with meat or fish.

Time: 25 minutes

⅔ cup uncooked rice
1 onion, sliced thin
2 teaspoons salt

1 cup fresh or frozen peas, cooked
¼ cup (4 tablespoons) butter

Cook the rice and onion in 2 cups of salted water until onion is tender and rice is dry and flaky. Mix with the cooked peas and butter. Heat briefly and serve. Makes 4 servings.

SPINACH RICE

Time: 12 or 13 minutes

¼ cup chopped onion
3 tablespoons butter or other fat
1 package (1⅓ cups) precooked rice

1 teaspoon salt
pepper
½ cup chopped cooked spinach
½ cup grated Parmesan cheese

Sauté onion in butter or fat until golden. Cook rice with salt according to directions on the package. Add spinach, onions, pepper, and sprinkle with cheese. Heat briefly over low flame until spinach is hot and cheese is melted. Makes 4 servings.

GREEN RICE

A delicately savory dish to serve with an important meat.

Time: 45 minutes

½ cup olive oil
½ bunch green or spring
   onions, tops and bottoms
   chopped
1 large green pepper, seeds removed, diced
1 cup uncooked rice

2 cups chicken broth or bouillon
1 cup grated Swiss cheese
½ bunch watercress, leaves
   only
salt, pepper

Sauté the onions, tops and bottoms, in the olive oil until pale yellow. Add the green pepper and the rice. Stir until the rice is well coated. Transfer to a casserole and mix in the chicken broth, the cheese, watercress, and seasoning. Cover and bake in a 325° oven for 35 minutes or until the rice is tender and flaky and the liquid all absorbed. Serve immediately. Makes 4 servings.

RICE WITH PIMIENTOS

This is simple, colorful, and knee deep in vitamins.

Time: 5 minutes

2 cups hot, flaky cooked rice
4 canned pimientos, chopped
   and drained
2 tablespoons butter

¼ cup hot chicken or beef
   broth or bouillon
salt, freshly ground pepper

Sauté the pimientos in the butter briefly and then add the bouillon and swish around the pan a minute. Pour over the rice and stir slightly with a fork. Add lots of salt and pepper. Serve immediately. Makes 4 servings.

RISOTTO ALLA MILANESE
Italy

When the Italians serve rice with a main meat dish, it is this classic and wonderful version.

Time: 45 minutes

1 cup uncooked rice
¼ cup butter
1 small onion, chopped fine
½ cup Marsala
4 cups chicken broth (or 4 cubes dissolved in 4 cups of water)

salt, pepper
½ teaspoon saffron, steeped in ¼ cup hot water
1 cup grated Parmesan or Romano cheese

Wash the rice in several waters. Melt half the butter in a heavy deep skillet and sauté the onion until a nice golden brown. Add the rice and stir constantly for about 10 minutes until the rice is well coated and translucent. Add the wine and half the broth. Bring to a boil, then turn flame down low and simmer for about 20 minutes, adding more broth as necessary and stirring occasionally to keep from sticking. When almost done, add the rest of the butter and salt and pepper (depending on the seasoning of the broth). Add the dissolved saffron. Serve with the cheese sprinkled on top. Makes 4 servings.

BAKED PILAF

Time: 35 minutes

⅔ stick butter
1 plump clove garlic, minced
1 cup uncooked long-grain rice

2 cups bouillon
salt, if needed

Sauté the garlic and rice in the butter until pale yellow. Turn into a casserole, add 1 cup bouillon. Cover and bake 15 minutes. Add the other cup of bouillon and bake 15 minutes more or until the liquid is absorbed and the rice tender. Makes 4 servings.

CHICKEN RICE

This is a delicate and bland accompaniment to meat and green vegetables.

Time: 20 minutes

1 package (1⅓ cups) pre-
cooked rice
1½ cups milk
½ teaspoon salt

dash of pepper
1 can (10½ oz.) condensed
cream of chicken soup

Combine precooked rice, milk, salt, and pepper in saucepan, and cook the rice according to directions on the package (using the milk as the liquid, of course). Add chicken soup and reheat. Makes 4 servings.

SAFFRON RICE

Time: 20 minutes

⅓ cup butter
¾ cup chopped onions
4 cups (15-oz. package) pre-
cooked rice

4 cups chicken broth
1¼ teaspoons salt
⅛ teaspoon pepper
⅛ teaspoon saffron

Melt butter in saucepan, add onion, and sauté over low heat until tender but not browned. Add rice, chicken broth, salt, pepper, and saffron. Mix just until all rice is moistened. Bring quickly to a boil over high heat, uncovered, fluffing rice gently once or twice with a fork (do *not* stir). Boil 2 minutes. Cover and remove from heat. Let stand 10 minutes. Makes 8 servings.

QUICK BROWNED RICE

This is a savory rice to be served as a vegetable course. It is good with almost any meat, fish, or fowl.

Time: 25 minutes

2 cups chicken broth
¼ teaspoon onion salt
¼ teaspoon celery salt
⅛ teaspoon pepper

1 teaspoon Kitchen Bouquet
1 cup uncooked rice, long-
grain or converted type

Put chicken broth, onion salt, celery salt, pepper and Kitchen Bouquet in saucepan. Cover and bring to boil. Stir in rice and cook, covered, over low heat until rice is tender—about 20 minutes. Makes 4 servings.

CUSTARDY RICE RING

Fill the center of this—or Buttered Rice Ring—with creamed shrimp and sliced okra, sprinkled with a tablespoon of grated lemon peel; creamed crabmeat sprinkled with slivered sautéed almonds; creamed diced chicken and mushrooms with a tablespoon of capers strewn on top; or lobster and slivered almonds in a mushroom sauce.

Time: 1 hour

½ cup milk
¾ cup grated Parmesan or Swiss cheese
2 eggs
½ cup minced parsley

1 small onion, chopped fine
½ teaspoon Worcestershire sauce
salt
3 cups hot cooked rice

Beat the eggs slightly, mix with milk, the grated cheese, parsley, and onion. Season with the Worcestershire sauce and salt. Mix into the rice, place in a buttered ring mold, and bake in a 350° oven for 45 minutes. Makes 4 servings.

BUTTERED RICE RING

Time: 20 minutes

1 package (1⅓ cups) pre-cooked rice

½ teaspoon salt
2 tablespoons butter

Cook rice, with salt, according to directions on the package. Add butter, fluff gently with a fork, and pack in a well-buttered 7-inch ring mold. Let stand a few minutes. Turn out onto hot platter. Makes 4 servings.

See recipe for Custardy Rice Ring for suggestions for serving.

9. STUFFINGS, BREADS, FRITTERS, COOKIES

RICE WINE STUFFING

A light and delicate concoction to embellish any chicken.

Time: 20 minutes

¼ cup currants
1 package (1⅓ cups) pre-
  cooked rice
¾ cup dry sherry
½ teaspoon salt
dash of pepper

⅛ teaspoon nutmeg
¼ teaspoon cardamon
⅛ teaspoon allspice
1 teaspoon sugar
¼ cup butter
¼ cup chopped almonds

Cover currants with water, bring to a boil, remove from heat, and let stand about 5 minutes. Drain. Combine rice and 1 cup water in saucepan. Mix just until all rice is moistened. Bring quickly to a boil over high heat, uncovered, fluffing rice gently once or twice with a fork. (Do *not* stir.) Add sherry, salt, pepper, nutmeg, cardamon, allspice, sugar, and currants. Cover and remove from heat. Let stand 10 minutes. Melt butter in skillet, and sauté the almonds in it until lightly browned, stirring constantly. Add to rice mixture. Makes 3 cups stuffing, or enough for a 4-pound dressed roasting chicken.

PARCHED RICE DRESSING

One of the best ways of cooking rice is to parch it first so that it is golden brown with a dry, somewhat nutty flavor. This way makes a good dressing too. It's a Chinese-Hawaiian trick.

Time: 45 minutes

½ cup uncooked rice
3 tablespoons butter or margarine
1 tablespoon minced onion
1 tablespoon minced parsley

⅓ cup minced celery
1 egg, well beaten
1 cup fine breadcrumbs, toasted
salt, pepper

Spread the rice in a dry skillet and put over a low flame. Watch carefully, shaking from time to time, until all the rice is an even brown. Put in a saucepan with 1 cup cold water and 1 teaspoon salt. Cover and set over a hot flame until the water boils, then turn the flame as low as possible and simmer for 14 minutes more. Remove the lid and let the rice dry out.

Melt the butter or margarine, and sauté the onion, parsley, and celery in it until tender. Mix with rice, egg, crumbs, and seasoning. Stuff lightly into the bird, being careful not to pack it. Makes about 3 cups.

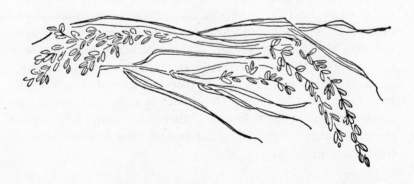

SAUSAGE STUFFING

This is a robust and yet light dressing. The mushrooms and celery leaves give an especially pleasing minor touch.

Time: 25 minutes

¼ lb. sausage
1 tablespoon butter
¼ cup chopped onion
¼ lb. mushrooms, chopped
1 package (1⅓ cups) pre-
   cooked rice
1 cup diced celery

¼ cup chopped celery leaves
1½ teaspoon salt
⅛ teaspoon pepper
¼ teaspoon savory
⅛ teaspoon thyme
⅛ teaspoon sage

Brown sausage. Add butter, onion, and mushrooms. Sauté for 3 minutes. Add remaining ingredients and 1½ cups water. Mix just until all rice is moistened. Bring quickly to a boil over high heat, uncovered, fluffing rice gently once or twice with a fork—do *not* stir. Cover and remove from heat. Let stand 10 minutes. Makes 4⅔ cups stuffing, or enough for a 5-pound roasting chicken.

DRIED FRUIT STUFFING
FOR DUCK

This is from a rather serious Moslem, a Somali from Ethiopia, who works for the U.N. The wine sounds wrong for his religion, but Jan Kindler, a friend of his, says the rules are not as strict as one thinks. Originally this was a stuffing for a lamb, but it has been modified for duck. It may also be used to stuff eggplant.

Time: 15 minutes

3 tablespoons butter
1 plump clove garlic, minced
1 medium-sized onion, chopped
1 medium-sized sweet green pepper, chopped
1½ cups cooked rice
⅓ box mixed dried fruits, chopped but not cooked
⅓ cup chopped dates and walnuts
½ cup white wine
salt
paprika
cinnamon

Sauté the garlic, onion, and pepper in the butter until slightly cooked. Add rice. Stir until all the vegetables are well cooked. Add chopped fruits, dates and walnuts, wine, and seasoning. Fill duck—or scooped-out halves of eggplant—with rice mixture, being careful not to pack too tightly. Roast the duck—or bake the eggplant in a pan with about an inch of water in the bottom. Makes enough to stuff 1 duck.

WILD RICE AND OYSTER STUFFING

Wild rice is as good as it is expensive, and that is extravagant praise. Long Island duckling—what one gets in stores—is a more sensible price, which counteracts that of the rice. This stuffing would be especially fine with any wild ducks you might have given to you.

Time: 10 minutes

2 cups cooked wild rice
1 small onion, chopped fine
2 strips crisp cooked bacon,
   crumbled coarsely
pinch of sage

pinch of thyme
2 tablespoons finely minced
   parsley
1 pint oysters and their liquor
salt, pepper

Mix all the ingredients together and stuff them into the bird. Fasten the openings with poultry skewers—or, less aesthetically, by sewing with string—and roast the duck.

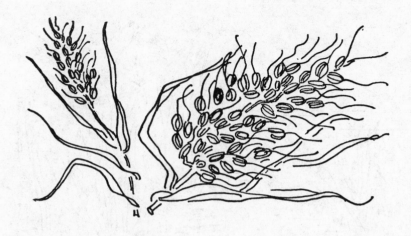

RICE SPOONBREAD

This is one of the good things to do with excess cooked rice. It is a pleasing variant on the usual spoonbread. Butter it generously and serve it—with a spoon, naturally—in place of potatoes, rice, pasta or hot bread.

Time: 1 hour

2 eggs, separated
1 cup white cornmeal
2 cups cooked rice
1 cup milk

3 tablespoons melted butter
salt
dash of sugar (about ½ tea-spoon)

Beat the egg yolks. Pour 1 cup boiling water over the cornmeal to scald. Mix the rice, the cornmeal, and milk with the egg yolks. Add melted butter, salt, and sugar. Whip the egg whites until stiff and fold in gently. Pour into a greased baking dish and bake in a 350° oven for 45 to 55 minutes, or until a pretty brown. Makes 4 to 6 servings.

RICE BREAD MADE WITH YEAST

Bread, beautiful and translucent, unlike any from the baker. Serve spread with softened cream cheese and marmalade for tea.

Time: 3 to 4 hours

½ cup milk, scalded
⅓ cup shortening, preferably butter
⅓ cup sugar
1 teaspoon salt

7 cups cooked rice
½ cake compressed yeast
¼ cup milk, slightly warmed
8 cups bread flour, sifted twice
melted butter for the top

Put the scalded milk, shortening, sugar, and salt in a pan and heat until the butter is melted. Cool to lukewarm and add to the rice. Dissolve the yeast in warm milk and stir into the rice. Work in the flour gradually, blending each time it is added. There should be enough flour to make a rather firm dough. Knead on a floured board until the dough feels satiny and smooth. Put in a greased bowl or bread trough, cover with a clean towel, and let stand in a warm but not hot place until the dough has doubled its size. Knead it again for several minutes. Divide into 2 parts, shape into 2 loaves, and put into 2 greased bread pans. Let rise until double in bulk. Brush the tops with melted butter. Bake in a 375° oven for 50 to 60 minutes.

ORANGE RICE MUFFINS

Time: 45 minutes

2 cups sifted flour
2½ teaspoons double-action baking powder
3 tablespoons sugar
¾ teaspoon salt
3 tablespoons grated orange peel

1 whole egg and 1 egg yolk, beaten
¾ cup boiled rice
1 cup milk
2 tablespoons melted butter

Sift the flour, baking powder, sugar, and salt together. Add the orange peel. Mix the beaten eggs thoroughly with the rice, and then add the milk and beat until well mixed. Add the dry ingredients gradually and beat well. Add the melted butter. Bake in buttered muffin tins at 425° for about 25 to 30 minutes or until done. Makes about 30 muffins.

RICE GRIDDLE CAKES
New Orleans

In New Orleans these are served in the afternoon with a light, sharp white wine and powdered sugar—at a time when other people are rashly drinking cocktails.

Time: 45 minutes

1 pint milk
1½ cups cold boiled rice
2 eggs, separated, yolks and whites beaten

1½ teaspoons salt
3 tablespoons baking powder
1½ cups flour

Scald the milk and set it to cool. Press the rice through a sieve, then add the well-beaten egg yolks, then the salt, baking powder, and flour. Blend and beat well. Add the milk, beating until thoroughly blended, and finally fold in the whites of the eggs, beaten to a stiff froth. Mix thoroughly, drop by spoonfuls on a hot griddle, and bake. Makes 4 to 6 servings.

SOUTHERN RICE BATTER CAKES

Another pancake that is as good with tea or white wine in the afternoon as for breakfast or lunch. At lunchtime serve with sour cream and red caviar—this is a most unorthodox suggestion and has nothing to do with the South, but the flavors are good.

Time: ½ hour

½ cup uncooked rice
½ teaspoon salt
1½ cups milk

1 tablespoon white cornmeal
1 egg, beaten

Cook washed and salted rice in boiling milk in double boiler until soft and mushy. Add cornmeal just before rice has finished cooking. Mix thoroughly and then cool. When cold, add the well-beaten egg. Fry in small cakes on a greased griddle, browning on both sides. Makes 4 to 6 servings.

RICE FRITTERS

Serve with roast chicken or turkey, cranberry sauce, and a bowl of chilled plum tomatoes, cauliflower flowerlets, and thin strips of green pepper.

Time: ½ hour

3 cups cooked rice, mashed
3 eggs
½ cup flour

sugar to taste
fat for frying
powdered sugar

Mix all ingredients except fat and powdered sugar into a light thick batter. Drop by tablespoonfuls into hot deep fat heated to 375° or 385°, and fry until golden brown. Sprinkle with powdered sugar. Makes 4 to 6 servings.

DANISH RICE FRITTERS

Serve these as dessert, sprinkled with powdered sugar, and with a bowl of jam to spoon over them.

Time: ½ hour

2 cups cold boiled rice
2 eggs
⅓ cup seedless raisins
1 tablespoon grated lemon rind

¼ cup chopped almonds
2 tablespoons flour
¼ cup butter
powdered sugar

Mix the rice, eggs, grated lemon rind, chopped almonds, raisins, and flour. Heat butter to 375° or 385° in skillet. Drop rice mixture by spoonfuls into pan and fry on both sides. Sprinkle with powdered sugar and serve with jam. Makes 4 to 6 servings.

CALAS
New Orleans

Through the streets of New Orleans, Negro women, crying, *"Belle calas, tout chaud,"* used to carry these cakes—piping hot, wrapped in clean towels in baskets. The calas are eaten with café au lait for breakfast.

Time: 12 hours

½ cup uncooked rice   3 tablespoons flour
½ cake compressed yeast   ½ teaspoon nutmeg
3 eggs, beaten   lard or other fat
½ cup sugar   powdered sugar

Wash rice thoroughly and put it into 3 cups boiling water. Boil until mushy. Cool. Dissolve yeast in ½ cup lukewarm water. When the rice is cold, mash well and mix with yeast. Let the dough rise overnight. In the morning add the well-beaten eggs and mix well. Add sugar and flour and beat thoroughly. Let rise for 15 minutes. Add nutmeg and beat again.

Fry in deep fat (lard) by dropping the dough in, a large spoonful at a time. Fry to a golden brown, remove, and drain on brown paper. Sprinkle with powdered sugar and eat while still warm.

米

食品名饌頁　　粉

陝 飯 賴 天
中國果品

HONG YEN BEANG (ALMOND COOKIES)
China

Time: 1 hour

½ cup butter
½ cup sugar
2 eggs

2 cups rice flour
few drops almond extract
24 blanched almonds

Cream butter with the sugar. Add the eggs and gradually work
in the rice flour. Add almond extract, knead well, and chill for 30
minutes. Form into balls about 1 inch in diameter, flatten with the
palm of your hand, and press one blanched almond in the center
of each cooky. Bake in a 350° oven for about 25 minutes or until
straw-colored. Makes about 2 dozen cookies.

10. DESSERTS

CRÈME DE RIZ (RICE CREAM)

This pudding is one that those who take a serious and sensual delight in food eat blissfully in their dreams; yet it is simple enough for children.

Time: 3¼ hours

4 cups milk
¼ cup uncooked rice
⅓ cup sugar
1 piece of vanilla bean about 1 inch long (or ½ teaspoon vanilla extract)

½ teaspoon salt
1 jigger Grand Marnier or Curaçao
3 tablespoons heavy cream

Mix the milk, rice, sugar, salt, and vanilla bean (if you are using it—do *not* add the extract now) in a shallow baking dish. Put in a very low oven, about 300°, and bake for about 3 hours or until the rice is dissolved and the mixture is a smooth and unctuous cream. Remove the vanilla bean—or add the extract at this time if bean has not been used. Add the Grand Marnier or Curaçao—but not if this is for children. Whip slightly with a wire whisk. Chill until very cold and add the cream. Whip a little more before serving. Makes 6 to 8 servings.

SWEDISH RICE DESSERT
WITH CHERRY SAUCE

A rich and creamy dish, gently contrasted with a pretty and delicately acid sauce.

Time: 1½ hours

½ package (⅔ cup) pre-cooked rice
2 cups milk
½ teaspoon salt
2 tablespoons sugar
¼ cup chopped blanched almonds
½ teaspoon vanilla
1 cup heavy cream, whipped

SAUCE

1 No. 2½ can pitted Bing cherries, drained
1½ cups cherry juice
5 tablespoons cornstarch

Combine rice and milk in saucepan. Mix just until all rice is moistened. Cook, covered, over low heat 15 minutes, fluffing rice occasionally with a fork. Remove from heat; add salt, sugar, almonds, and vanilla. Chill. Fold in whipped cream. Chill 20 minutes longer. Serve with warm cherry sauce. Makes 6 servings.

To make the sauce, blend 2 tablespoons cherry juice with cornstarch. Combine remaining juice and cornstarch mixture in saucepan. Cook until thickened and clear—about 5 minutes—stirring constantly. Remove from heat. Add cherries. Serve warm. Makes about 3 cups sauce.

CARAMEL RICE PUDDING

This is crème brûlée with rice added.

Time: 1¼ hours

1¼ cups sugar	2 eggs
1 cup uncooked rice	1 egg yolk
3 cups milk	1 teaspoon vanilla extract
4 tablespoons butter	

Carmelize a mold as follows: Heat ½ cup of the sugar in a heavy iron skillet until it becomes dark brown. Pour this into a mold (a ring mold is pleasing), and rotate the mold rapidly and constantly until the sides and bottom are completely covered with the caramel (hold the mold in a towel during this process, because it can get awfully hot). Wash the rice and then boil it for 2 minutes in enough water to cover. Drain thoroughly. Bring the milk to a boil, add the rice, and cook for about 20 minutes or until rice is tender. Beat the eggs and the egg yolk with the remaining sugar and the butter until light and yellow. Stir into the rice and add the vanilla. Put into the caramelized mold. Set the mold in a pan containing hot water about 1 inch deep, and bake for 35 minutes in a 350° oven, or until a silver knife inserted in the center comes out clean. Remove from the oven and allow to cool. When it is lukewarm, unmold onto a serving plate. Chill. Serve cold. Makes 6 to 8 servings.

RICE PUDDING WITH FIGS AND GINGER

Not at all like the nursery version. Serve this to tired sophisticates after a highly seasoned meal.

Time: 1¼ hours

½ package dried figs
1 cup cooked rice
¼ cup honey

3 tablespoons finely minced preserved ginger
½ cup heavy cream

Simmer the figs until tender—about ½ hour—and chop. Mix the rice with the honey. Stir in the chopped cooked figs and the preserved ginger. Whip the cream until stiff and gently fold it in. Chill for about an hour before serving. Makes 4 servings.

LEMON RICE PUDDING

Time: 20 minutes

¾ cup precooked rice
2½ cups milk
1 egg, slightly beaten
⅓ cup sugar

½ teaspoon salt
1 tablespoon lemon juice
1 teaspoon grated lemon rind
1 tablespoon butter

Put milk and rice in saucepan and bring to a full boil. Remove from heat and let stand 10 minutes. Combine egg, sugar, salt, lemon juice, and rind. Add a small amount of the rice mixture, stir well, and put in the saucepan with the rice. Add butter and cook about 4 minutes, stirring constantly. Serve warm, with cream if desired. Makes 4 servings.

CHINESE RICE PUDDING

In the traditional version the rice, fruit, and nuts are arranged in layers that unmold decoratively, and the pudding is called "Eight Jewels." The directions given here are adapted to American ways of doing the same thing in a slightly lazier fashion.

Time: 1½ to 2 hours

1 cup uncooked rice
2 teaspoons sugar
½ teaspoon salt
2 tablespoons sweet butter
½ cup dates, lichee nuts, or candied fruits, chopped coarsely

½ cup Chinese almonds or walnuts (or plain almonds), chopped
extra almonds or walnuts, for garnishing

Bring 2 cups water to a boil, add the rice, sugar, salt, and butter. Cover and simmer over low flame for about 30 minutes or until rice is tender and liquid absorbed. Mix with the nuts and fruits and put into a well-buttered mold. Steam about 20 minutes in a pan containing an inch of water, or in a pressure cooker for about 2 minutes under 15 pounds pressure. Chill. Unmold, sprinkle with extra almonds or walnuts, and serve. Makes 4 servings.

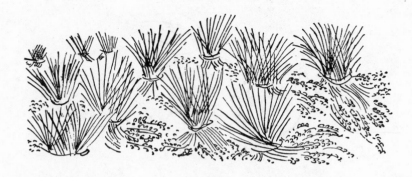

RIZOGALO
Greece

This is still rice pudding made the usual way, but the honey, grated orange peel, and cinnamon and nutmeg give it a delicate and subtle flavor.

Time: 1 hour

4 cups milk
¼ cup uncooked rice
4 tablespoons honey

grated rind of 1 orange
cinnamon
nutmeg

Scald the milk and keep it hot. Bring 1 cup of the scalded milk to a boil, add the rice, and cook over low heat, stirring constantly. Add more milk from time to time as it is absorbed, until all is used. This should take from 40 to 50 minutes. At the end of 30 minutes add the grated orange rind and the honey. When all the milk is absorbed, pour into serving dish and dust with cinnamon and a few specks of freshly ground nutmeg.

Some recipes add 2 egg yolks, which are stirred into the rice when it has slightly cooled. Others call for the addition of a few drops of oil of orange blossoms. Makes 4 to 6 servings.

BAVARIAN RICE PUDDING

Time: 1½ hours

½ package (⅔ cup) pre-
cooked rice
1 envelope unflavored gelatin
¼ cup granulated sugar
1 teaspoon brown sugar
½ teaspoon salt
¼ teaspoon nutmeg

1¼ cups milk
1 egg, slightly beaten
⅛ teaspoon vanilla
¼ cup chopped citron
2 teaspoons lemon juice
1 teaspoon grated lemon rind
1 cup cream, whipped

Prepare precooked rice as directed on package. Cool. Soften gelatin in ¼ cup cold water. Combine sugars, salt, nutmeg, and gelatin in top of double boiler. Add milk and egg and mix well. Place over hot water and cook, stirring constantly until mixture coats spoon. Add vanilla, citron, lemon juice, and lemon rind. Chill until slightly thickened. Then fold in rice and whipped cream, and chill in sherbet glasses. Makes 8 servings.

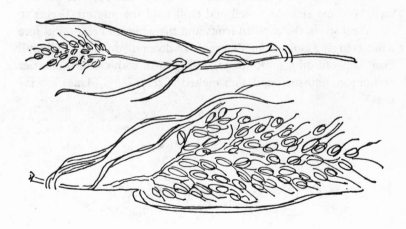

JIM BEARD'S RIZ À L'IMPÉRATRICE

This is Jim's version of the most beautiful, intricate, and elegant of all rice puddings, suitable for a truly important occasion.

Time: 3 to 4 hours

1 cup mixed candied fruits, finely chopped (preferably from a fancy grocery store)
¼ cup brandy
½ cup uncooked rice
1¼ cups milk
1 cup hot milk
4 egg yolks

⅔ cup sugar
1 teaspoon vanilla
1 tablespoon unflavored gelatin
1 cup heavy cream, whipped
candied cherries
currant jelly, melted
citron

Soak the fruit in brandy for 30 minutes. Wash the rice in cold water, put in a saucepan, and cover with cold water. Bring to a boil and simmer just 2 minutes. Drain and rinse with cold water. Put back in the saucepan with 1¼ cups milk, and let cook about 20 minutes or until the rice is tender. Put hot milk in double boiler over boiling water; stir in egg yolks and sugar. Cook and stir with wooden spoon or whisk until smooth and thick. Add vanilla. Dissolve the gelatin in 2 tablespoons cold water, and stir into the custard. Add the rice. Mix well and chill until the mixture begins to set. Then stir in the candied fruits and the whipped cream. Put into a buttered ring mold or another mold of decorative shape. Chill until firm. Unmold on a pretty plate, and garnish with candied cherries and citron, and surround with melted currant jelly. Makes 6 servings.

DATE RICE CUSTARD

Time: 45 minutes

½ package (⅔ cup) pre-
cooked rice
3 cups milk
2 eggs, slightly beaten
½ cup sugar
½ teaspoon salt

½ teaspoon vanilla
¼ teaspoon nutmeg
¼ cup chopped pecan meats
¼ cup chopped dates
1 tablespoon butter

Combine rice and milk in saucepan. Mix just until all rice is moistened. Bring quickly to a boil over high heat, uncovered, fluffing rice gently once or twice with a fork. (Do *not* stir.) Remove from heat. Put aside, uncovered, so that the rice will cool slightly.

Mix the eggs, sugar, salt, vanilla, and nutmeg. Add hot rice mixture gradually and mix thoroughly. Gently stir in pecan meats, dates, and butter. Turn into greased 1½-quart baking dish. Place in pan of hot water and bake in moderate oven (375°) for 35 minutes, stirring once after 5 minutes and again after 10 minutes. Serve with plain or whipped cream, foamy sauce, or custard sauce. Makes 6 servings.

BAKED APPLES IN RICE CUSTARD

This simple yet distinguished and nutritious recipe turns up in different versions in Canadian, Southern, and French cookbooks— the common denominator being, of course, the French strain.

Time: 2 hours (more if chilled)

4 plump apples, as nearly the same size as possible, peeled and cored
4 tablespoons brown sugar
2 tablespoons finely chopped citron
1 tablespoon butter

3 cups milk
¾ cup sugar
pinch of salt
2 whole eggs, 1 egg yolk, slightly beaten
1 jigger rum
1 cup cooked rice

Put the apples in a shallow casserole, and fill the center of each with brown sugar and chopped citron and a piece of butter. Pour ¼ cup water in the bottom of the dish. Bake in a medium (350°) oven for 45 minutes or longer, until the apples are tender but not mushy. Remove from the oven. Scald the milk with the sugar and salt. Pour slowly over the beaten eggs and beat until well blended. Add rum and stir. Mix in the cooked rice and pour over the baked apples. Set the casserole in a pan of hot water (about 1 inch deep). Bake in a 350° oven for about one hour or until a silver knife inserted comes out clean, and the top is lightly browned. Makes 4 generous servings.

NUT PILAF
Turkey

This may be served hot or cold, either as a dessert or with meat.

Time: 1¼ hours

1 cup uncooked rice
½ cup milk
½ cup pistachio nuts or
chopped almonds
⅓ cup chopped dates

2 tablespoons grated orange
peel
2 tablespoons granulated sugar
2 tablespoons melted butter

Cook the rice, according to basic directions, until tender but not mushy. Drain. Put in shallow buttered casserole with milk and other ingredients. Stir and mix. Cover, set in 1 inch water in a pan, and steam for about 1 hour in a 350° oven. Serve hot or cold as a dessert or with meat. Makes 4 servings.

APRICOT RICE

Time: 25 minutes if served warm; 1¼ hours if chilled

¾ cup precooked rice
2 cups apricot nectar
3 tablespoons sugar
⅛ teaspoon salt

½ teaspoon almond extract
1 tablespoon butter
whipped cream

Combine rice and nectar, sugar and salt. Bring to a full boil. Cover and simmer 5 minutes. Remove from heat, cover, and let stand 10 minutes. Add almond extract and butter. Serve warm or chilled with whipped cream. Makes 4 servings.

RASPBERRY RICE

A faster, simpler, and less stable version of this may be made by mixing cold cooked rice, whipped cream, and drained sweetened raspberries just before serving.

Time: 2 to 3 hours

⅔ cup frozen raspberries (or strawberries)
1 envelope unflavored gelatin
½ cup heavy cream
3 cups cold cooked rice

1 jigger Framboise (French raspberry liqueur), Curaçao, or Cointreau—nice but not obligatory

Drain the berries, but save the juice. Soften the gelatin in ¼ cup juice. Whip the ice-cold cream until it "peaks" or holds its shape. Mix rice with raspberries or strawberries and liqueur, if you are using it. Heat the rest of the juice, and dissolve the softened gelatin in it. Mix with rice and berry mixture. Fold the whipped cream in gently. Chill in pretty glass bowl or individual sherbet glasses until ready to serve—or put in a mold, unmold, and decorate. Makes 4 servings.

RICE CROQUETTES WITH FRUIT
New Orleans

From Owen Brennan's French and Creole Restaurant in New Orleans.

Time: 45 minutes

1 pint milk
½ cup uncooked rice
2 egg yolks, beaten
2 heaping tablespoons sugar
½ teaspoon vanilla extract
¼ cup seeded raisins
¼ cup currants

¼ cup chopped citron
1 egg, beaten
breadcrumbs
fat for frying
currant jelly
powdered sugar

Put the milk into a double boiler and add the rice. Boil until rice is tender and has absorbed almost all the milk. Add the beaten egg yolks to the rice, and then stir in the sugar. Beat until very smooth, then take the mixture off the stove and add the vanilla, raisins, currants, and citron. Put in a bowl and cool. Mold into croquettes. Dip each piece into the well-beaten egg and then into breadcrumbs. Fry in bubbling hot fat. Drain well, and when ready to serve put a piece of currant jelly on top of each croquette and dust the whole with powdered sugar. May be served with a vanilla sauce. Makes 4 to 6 servings.

FRUIT AU VIN IN RICE RING

Serve this for a buffet supper when you are arranging the table to look like the beautiful color photographs in the slick magazines.

Time: 45 minutes

2½ tablespoons cornstarch
½ cup sugar
dash of salt
1 cup dry sherry or rum
2 to 3 tablespoons lemon juice
1 cup sliced fresh peaches
1 cup halved seeded Malaga or Tokay grapes

1 package (1⅓ cups) pre-cooked rice
2⅓ cups milk
½ teaspoon salt
3 tablespoons sugar
¼ teaspoon nutmeg
2 tablespoons butter

To make the Fruit au Vin, combine cornstarch, sugar, and dash of salt in saucepan. Add ¾ cup cold water gradually, blending well. Cook and stir over medium heat until mixture comes to a boil and is thickened and clear. Remove from heat; add sherry or rum and lemon juice, mixing well. Then add fruit. Chill thoroughly. Makes 4 cups fruit sauce.

Combine rice, milk, and salt in large saucepan. Mix just until all rice is moistened. Bring to a boil. Boil gently, loosely covered, 15 minutes, fluffing rice occasionally with a fork. Remove from heat and add sugar, nutmeg, and butter; mix lightly. Pack in a well-greased 1-quart ring mold. Let stand 5 to 10 minutes, or during supper. Unmold on large platter. Fill center of ring with Fruit au Vin, or use 1 jar brandied black Bing cherries with 4 ounces slivered almonds. Makes 10 servings.

INDEX

A CATALOGUE OF
SELECTED DOVER BOOKS
IN ALL FIELDS OF INTEREST

A CATALOGUE OF SELECTED DOVER BOOKS IN ALL FIELDS OF INTEREST

CELESTIAL OBJECTS FOR COMMON TELESCOPES, T. W. Webb. The most used book in amateur astronomy: inestimable aid for locating and identifying nearly 4,000 celestial objects. Edited, updated by Margaret W. Mayall. 77 illustrations. Total of 645pp. 5⅜ x 8½.
20917-2, 20918-0 Pa., Two-vol. set $9.00

HISTORICAL STUDIES IN THE LANGUAGE OF CHEMISTRY, M. P. Crosland. The important part language has played in the development of chemistry from the symbolism of alchemy to the adoption of systematic nomenclature in 1892. ". . . wholeheartedly recommended,"—Science. 15 illustrations. 416pp. of text. 5⅝ x 8¼. 63702-6 Pa. $6.00

BURNHAM'S CELESTIAL HANDBOOK, Robert Burnham, Jr. Thorough, readable guide to the stars beyond our solar system. Exhaustive treatment, fully illustrated. Breakdown is alphabetical by constellation: Andromeda to Cetus in Vol. 1; Chamaeleon to Orion in Vol. 2; and Pavo to Vulpecula in Vol. 3. Hundreds of illustrations. Total of about 2000pp. 6⅛ x 9¼.
23567-X, 23568-8, 23673-0 Pa., Three-vol. set $26.85

THEORY OF WING SECTIONS: INCLUDING A SUMMARY OF AIRFOIL DATA, Ira H. Abbott and A. E. von Doenhoff. Concise compilation of subatomic aerodynamic characteristics of modern NASA wing sections, plus description of theory. 350pp. of tables. 693pp. 5⅜ x 8½.
60586-8 Pa. $7.00

DE RE METALLICA, Georgius Agricola. Translated by Herbert C. Hoover and Lou H. Hoover. The famous Hoover translation of greatest treatise on technological chemistry, engineering, geology, mining of early modern times (1556). All 289 original woodcuts. 638pp. 6¾ x 11.
60006-8 Clothbd. $17.50

THE ORIGIN OF CONTINENTS AND OCEANS, Alfred Wegener. One of the most influential, most controversial books in science, the classic statement for continental drift. Full 1966 translation of Wegener's final (1929) version. 64 illustrations. 246pp. 5⅜ x 8½. 61708-4 Pa. $3.00

THE PRINCIPLES OF PSYCHOLOGY, William James. Famous long course complete, unabridged. Stream of thought, time perception, memory, experimental methods; great work decades ahead of its time. Still valid, useful; read in many classes. 94 figures. Total of 1391pp. 5⅜ x 8½.
20381-6, 20382-4 Pa., Two-vol. set $13.00

YUCATAN BEFORE AND AFTER THE CONQUEST, Diego de Landa. First English translation of basic book in Maya studies, the only significant account of Yucatan written in the early post-Conquest era. Translated by distinguished Maya scholar William Gates. Appendices, introduction, 4 maps and over 120 illustrations added by translator. 162pp. 5⅜ x 8½.
23622-6 Pa. $3.00

THE MALAY ARCHIPELAGO, Alfred R. Wallace. Spirited travel account by one of founders of modern biology. Touches on zoology, botany, ethnography, geography, and geology. 62 illustrations, maps. 515pp. 5⅜ x 8½.
20187-2 Pa. $6.95

THE DISCOVERY OF THE TOMB OF TUTANKHAMEN, Howard Carter, A. C. Mace. Accompany Carter in the thrill of discovery, as ruined passage suddenly reveals unique, untouched, fabulously rich tomb. Fascinating account, with 106 illustrations. New introduction by J. M. White. Total of 382pp. 5⅜ x 8½. (Available in U.S. only) 23500-9 Pa. $4.00

THE WORLD'S GREATEST SPEECHES, edited by Lewis Copeland and Lawrence W. Lamm. Vast collection of 278 speeches from Greeks up to present. Powerful and effective models; unique look at history. Revised to 1970. Indices. 842pp. 5⅜ x 8½. 20468-5 Pa. $8.95

THE 100 GREATEST ADVERTISEMENTS, Julian Watkins. The priceless ingredient; His master's voice; 99 44/100% pure; over 100 others. How they were written, their impact, etc. Remarkable record. 130 illustrations. 233pp. 7⅞ x 10 3/5. 20540-1 Pa. $5.00

CRUICKSHANK PRINTS FOR HAND COLORING, George Cruickshank. 18 illustrations, one side of a page, on fine-quality paper suitable for watercolors. Caricatures of people in society (c. 1820) full of trenchant wit. Very large format. 32pp. 11 x 16. 23684-6 Pa. $5.00

THIRTY-TWO COLOR POSTCARDS OF TWENTIETH-CENTURY AMERICAN ART, Whitney Museum of American Art. Reproduced in full color in postcard form are 31 art works and one shot of the museum. Calder, Hopper, Rauschenberg, others. Detachable. 16pp. 8¼ x 11.
23629-3 Pa. $2.50

MUSIC OF THE SPHERES: THE MATERIAL UNIVERSE FROM ATOM TO QUASAR SIMPLY EXPLAINED, Guy Murchie. Planets, stars, geology, atoms, radiation, relativity, quantum theory, light, antimatter, similar topics. 319 figures. 664pp. 5⅜ x 8½.
21809-0, 21810-4 Pa., Two-vol. set $10.00

EINSTEIN'S THEORY OF RELATIVITY, Max Born. Finest semi-technical account; covers Einstein, Lorentz, Minkowski, and others, with much detail, much explanation of ideas and math not readily available elsewhere on this level. For student, non-specialist. 376pp. 5⅜ x 8½.
60769-0 Pa. $4.00

THE COMPLETE BOOK OF DOLL MAKING AND COLLECTING, Catherine Christopher. Instructions, patterns for dozens of dolls, from rag doll on up to elaborate, historically accurate figures. Mould faces, sew clothing, make doll houses, etc. Also collecting information. Many illustrations. 288pp. 6 x 9. 22066-4 Pa. $4.00

THE DAGUERREOTYPE IN AMERICA, Beaumont Newhall. Wonderful portraits, 1850's townscapes, landscapes; full text plus 104 photographs. The basic book. Enlarged 1976 edition. 272pp. 8¼ x 11¼. 23322-7 Pa. $6.00

CRAFTSMAN HOMES, Gustav Stickley. 296 architectural drawings, floor plans, and photographs illustrate 40 different kinds of "Mission-style" homes from *The Craftsman* (1901-16), voice of American style of simplicity and organic harmony. Thorough coverage of Craftsman idea in text and picture, now collector's item. 224pp. 8⅛ x 11. 23791-5 Pa. $6.00

PEWTER-WORKING: INSTRUCTIONS AND PROJECTS, Burl N. Osborn. & Gordon O. Wilber. Introduction to pewter-working for amateur craftsman. History and characteristics of pewter; tools, materials, step-by-step instructions. Photos, line drawings, diagrams. Total of 160pp. 7⅞ x 10¾. 23786-9 Pa. $3.50

THE GREAT CHICAGO FIRE, edited by David Lowe. 10 dramatic, eyewitness accounts of the 1871 disaster, including one of the aftermath and rebuilding, plus 70 contemporary photographs and illustrations of the ruins—courthouse, Palmer House, Great Central Depot, etc. Introduction by David Lowe. 87pp. 8¼ x 11. 23771-0 Pa. $4.00

SILHOUETTES: A PICTORIAL ARCHIVE OF VARIED ILLUSTRATIONS, edited by Carol Belanger Grafton. Over 600 silhouettes from the 18th to 20th centuries include profiles and full figures of men and women, children, birds and animals, groups and scenes, nature, ships, an alphabet. Dozens of uses for commercial artists and craftspeople. 144pp. 8⅜ x 11¼. 23781-8 Pa. $4.00

ANIMALS: 1,419 COPYRIGHT-FREE ILLUSTRATIONS OF MAMMALS, BIRDS, FISH, INSECTS, ETC., edited by Jim Harter. Clear wood engravings present, in extremely lifelike poses, over 1,000 species of animals. One of the most extensive copyright-free pictorial sourcebooks of its kind. Captions. Index. 284pp. 9 x 12. 23766-4 Pa. $7.50

INDIAN DESIGNS FROM ANCIENT ECUADOR, Frederick W. Shaffer. 282 original designs by pre-Columbian Indians of Ecuador (500-1500 A.D.). Designs include people, mammals, birds, reptiles, fish, plants, heads, geometric designs. Use as is or alter for advertising, textiles, leathercraft, etc. Introduction. 95pp. 8¾ x 11¼. 23764-8 Pa. $3.50

SZIGETI ON THE VIOLIN, Joseph Szigeti. Genial, loosely structured tour by premier violinist, featuring a pleasant mixture of reminiscenes, insights into great music and musicians, innumerable tips for practicing violinists. 385 musical passages. 256pp. 5⅝ x 8¼. 23763-X Pa. $3.50

TONE POEMS, SERIES II: TILL EULENSPIEGELS LUSTIGE STREICHE, ALSO SPRACH ZARATHUSTRA, AND EIN HELDEN-LEBEN, Richard Strauss. Three important orchestral works, including very popular *Till Eulenspiegel's Marry Pranks,* reproduced in full score from original editions. Study score. 315pp. 9⅜ x 12¼. (Available in U.S. only)
23755-9 Pa. $7.50

TONE POEMS, SERIES I: DON JUAN, TOD UND VERKLARUNG AND DON QUIXOTE, Richard Strauss. Three of the most often performed and recorded works in entire orchestral repertoire, reproduced in full score from original editions. Study score. 286pp. 9⅜ x 12¼. (Available in U.S. only)
23754-0 Pa. $7.50

11 LATE STRING QUARTETS, Franz Joseph Haydn. The form which Haydn defined and "brought to perfection." *(Grove's).* 11 string quartets in complete score, his last and his best. The first in a projected series of the complete Haydn string quartets. Reliable modern Eulenberg edition, otherwise difficult to obtain. 320pp. 8⅜ x 11¼. (Available in U.S. only)
23753-2 Pa. $6.95

FOURTH, FIFTH AND SIXTH SYMPHONIES IN FULL SCORE, Peter Ilyitch Tchaikovsky. Complete orchestral scores of Symphony No. 4 in F Minor, Op. 36; Symphony No. 5 in E Minor, Op. 64; Symphony No. 6 in B Minor, "Pathetique," Op. 74. Bretikopf & Hartel eds. Study score. 480pp. 9⅜ x 12¼. 23861-X Pa. $10.95

THE MARRIAGE OF FIGARO: COMPLETE SCORE, Wolfgang A. Mozart. Finest comic opera ever written. Full score, not to be confused with piano renderings. Peters edition. Study score. 448pp. 9⅜ x 12¼. (Available in U.S. only)
23751-6 Pa. $11.95

"IMAGE" ON THE ART AND EVOLUTION OF THE FILM, edited by Marshall Deutelbaum. Pioneering book brings together for first time 38 groundbreaking articles on early silent films from *Image* and 263 illustrations newly shot from rare prints in the collection of the International Museum of Photography. A landmark work. Index. 256pp. 8¼ x 11.
23777-X Pa. $8.95

AROUND-THE-WORLD COOKY BOOK, Lois Lintner Sumption and Marguerite Lintner Ashbrook. 373 cooky and frosting recipes from 28 countries (America, Austria, China, Russia, Italy, etc.) include Viennese kisses, rice wafers, London strips, lady fingers, hony, sugar spice, maple cookies, etc. Clear instructions. All tested. 38 drawings. 182pp. 5⅜ x 8.
23802-4 Pa. $2.50

THE ART NOUVEAU STYLE, edited by Roberta Waddell. 579 rare photographs, not available elsewhere, of works in jewelry, metalwork, glass, ceramics, textiles, architecture and furniture by 175 artists—Mucha, Seguy, Lalique, Tiffany, Gaudin, Hohlwein, Saarinen, and many others. 288pp. 8⅜ x 11¼. 23515-7 Pa. $6.95

THE AMERICAN SENATOR, Anthony Trollope. Little known, long unavailable Trollope novel on a grand scale. Here are humorous comment on American vs. English culture, and stunning portrayal of a heroine/villainess. Superb evocation of Victorian village life. 561pp. 5⅜ x 8½.
23801-6 Pa. $6.00

WAS IT MURDER? James Hilton. The author of *Lost Horizon* and *Goodbye, Mr. Chips* wrote one detective novel (under a pen-name) which was quickly forgotten and virtually lost, even at the height of Hilton's fame. This edition brings it back—a finely crafted public school puzzle resplendent with Hilton's stylish atmosphere. A thoroughly English thriller by the creator of Shangri-la. 252pp. 5⅜ x 8. (Available in U.S. only)
23774-5 Pa. $3.00

CENTRAL PARK: A PHOTOGRAPHIC GUIDE, Victor Laredo and Henry Hope Reed. 121 superb photographs show dramatic views of Central Park: Bethesda Fountain, Cleopatra's Needle, Sheep Meadow, the Blockhouse, plus people engaged in many park activities: ice skating, bike riding, etc. Captions by former Curator of Central Park, Henry Hope Reed, provide historical view, changes, etc. Also photos of N.Y. landmarks on park's periphery. 96pp. 8½ x 11.
23750-8 Pa. $4.50

NANTUCKET IN THE NINETEENTH CENTURY, Clay Lancaster. 180 rare photographs, stereographs, maps, drawings and floor plans recreate unique American island society. Authentic scenes of shipwreck, lighthouses, streets, homes are arranged in geographic sequence to provide walking-tour guide to old Nantucket existing today. Introduction, captions. 160pp. 8⅞ x 11¾.
23747-8 Pa. $6.95

STONE AND MAN: A PHOTOGRAPHIC EXPLORATION, Andreas Feininger. 106 photographs by *Life* photographer Feininger portray man's deep passion for stone through the ages. Stonehenge-like megaliths, fortified towns, sculpted marble and crumbling tenements show textures, beauties, fascination. 128pp. 9¼ x 10¾.
23756-7 Pa. $5.95

CIRCLES, A MATHEMATICAL VIEW, D. Pedoe. Fundamental aspects of college geometry, non-Euclidean geometry, and other branches of mathematics: representing circle by point. Poincare model, isoperimetric property, etc. Stimulating recreational reading. 66 figures. 96pp. 5⅝ x 8¼.
63698-4 Pa. $2.75

THE DISCOVERY OF NEPTUNE, Morton Grosser. Dramatic scientific history of the investigations leading up to the actual discovery of the eighth planet of our solar system. Lucid, well-researched book by well-known historian of science. 172pp. 5⅜ x 8½.
23726-5 Pa. $3.00

THE DEVIL'S DICTIONARY. Ambrose Bierce. Barbed, bitter, brilliant witticisms in the form of a dictionary. Best, most ferocious satire America has produced. 145pp. 5⅜ x 8½.
20487-1 Pa. $1.75

HISTORY OF BACTERIOLOGY, William Bulloch. The only comprehensive history of bacteriology from the beginnings through the 19th century. Special emphasis is given to biography-Leeuwenhoek, etc. Brief accounts of 350 bacteriologists form a separate section. No clearer, fuller study, suitable to scientists and general readers, has yet been written. 52 illustrations. 448pp. 5⅝ x 8¼.   23761-3 Pa. $6.50

THE COMPLETE NONSENSE OF EDWARD LEAR, Edward Lear. All nonsense limericks, zany alphabets, Owl and Pussycat, songs, nonsense botany, etc., illustrated by Lear. Total of 321pp. 5⅜ x 8½. (Available in U.S. only)   20167-8 Pa. $3.00

INGENIOUS MATHEMATICAL PROBLEMS AND METHODS, Louis A. Graham. Sophisticated material from Graham *Dial,* applied and pure; stresses solution methods. Logic, number theory, networks, inversions, etc. 237pp. 5⅜ x 8½.   20545-2 Pa. $3.50

BEST MATHEMATICAL PUZZLES OF SAM LOYD, edited by Martin Gardner. Bizarre, original, whimsical puzzles by America's greatest puzzler. From fabulously rare *Cyclopedia,* including famous 14-15 puzzles, the Horse of a Different Color, 115 more. Elementary math. 150 illustrations. 167pp. 5⅜ x 8½.   20498-7 Pa. $2.50

THE BASIS OF COMBINATION IN CHESS, J. du Mont. Easy-to-follow, instructive book on elements of combination play, with chapters on each piece and every powerful combination team—two knights, bishop and knight, rook and bishop, etc. 250 diagrams. 218pp. 5⅜ x 8½. (Available in U.S. only)   23644-7 Pa. $3.50

MODERN CHESS STRATEGY, Ludek Pachman. The use of the queen, the active king, exchanges, pawn play, the center, weak squares, etc. Section on rook alone worth price of the book. Stress on the moderns. Often considered the most important book on strategy. 314pp. 5⅜ x 8½.   20290-9 Pa. $3.50

LASKER'S MANUAL OF CHESS, Dr. Emanuel Lasker. Great world champion offers very thorough coverage of all aspects of chess. Combinations, position play, openings, end game, aesthetics of chess, philosophy of struggle, much more. Filled with analyzed games. 390pp. 5⅜ x 8½.   20640-8 Pa. $4.00

500 MASTER GAMES OF CHESS, S. Tartakower, J. du Mont. Vast collection of great chess games from 1798-1938, with much material nowhere else readily available. Fully annotated, arranged by opening for easier study. 664pp. 5⅜ x 8½.   23208-5 Pa. $6.00

A GUIDE TO CHESS ENDINGS, Dr. Max Euwe, David Hooper. One of the finest modern works on chess endings. Thorough analysis of the most frequently encountered endings by former world champion. 331 examples, each with diagram. 248pp. 5⅜ x 8½.   23332-4 Pa. $3.50

SECOND PIATIGORSKY CUP, edited by Isaac Kashdan. One of the greatest tournament books ever produced in the English language. All 90 games of the 1966 tournament, annotated by players, most annotated by both players. Features Petrosian, Spassky, Fischer, Larsen, six others. 228pp. 5⅜ x 8½.   23572-6 Pa. $3.50

ENCYCLOPEDIA OF CARD TRICKS, revised and edited by Jean Hugard. How to perform over 600 card tricks, devised by the world's greatest magicians: impromptus, spelling tricks, key cards, using special packs, much, much more. Additional chapter on card technique. 66 illustrations. 402pp. 5⅜ x 8½. (Available in U.S. only)   21252-1 Pa. $3.95

MAGIC: STAGE ILLUSIONS, SPECIAL EFFECTS AND TRICK PHOTOGRAPHY, Albert A. Hopkins, Henry R. Evans. One of the great classics; fullest, most authorative explanation of vanishing lady, levitations, scores of other great stage effects. Also small magic, automata, stunts. 446 illustrations. 556pp. 5⅜ x 8½.   23344-8 Pa. $5.00

THE SECRETS OF HOUDINI, J. C. Cannell. Classic study of Houdini's incredible magic, exposing closely-kept professional secrets and revealing, in general terms, the whole art of stage magic. 67 illustrations. 279pp. 5⅜ x 8½.   22913-0 Pa. $3.00

HOFFMANN'S MODERN MAGIC, Professor Hoffmann. One of the best, and best-known, magicians' manuals of the past century. Hundreds of tricks from card tricks and simple sleight of hand to elaborate illusions involving construction of complicated machinery. 332 illustrations. 563pp. 5⅜ x 8½.   23623-4 Pa. $6.00

MADAME PRUNIER'S FISH COOKERY BOOK, Mme. S. B. Prunier. More than 1000 recipes from world famous Prunier's of Paris and London, specially adapted here for American kitchen. Grilled tournedos with anchovy butter, Lobster a la Bordelaise, Prunier's prized desserts, more. Glossary. 340pp. 5⅜ x 8½. (Available in U.S. only)   22679-4 Pa. $3.00

FRENCH COUNTRY COOKING FOR AMERICANS, Louis Diat. 500 easy-to-make, authentic provincial recipes compiled by former head chef at New York's Fitz-Carlton Hotel: onion soup, lamb stew, potato pie, more. 309pp. 5⅜ x 8½.   23665-X Pa. $3.95

SAUCES, FRENCH AND FAMOUS, Louis Diat. Complete book gives over 200 specific recipes: bechamel, Bordelaise, hollandaise, Cumberland, apricot, etc. Author was one of this century's finest chefs, originator of vichyssoise and many other dishes. Index. 156pp. 5⅜ x 8.
                                                           23663-3 Pa. $2.50

TOLL HOUSE TRIED AND TRUE RECIPES, Ruth Graves Wakefield. Authentic recipes from the famous Mass. restaurant: popovers, veal and ham loaf, Toll House baked beans, chocolate cake crumb pudding, much more. Many helpful hints. Nearly 700 recipes. Index. 376pp. 5⅜ x 8½.
                                                           23560-2 Pa. $4.00

"OSCAR" OF THE WALDORF'S COOKBOOK, Oscar Tschirky. Famous American chef reveals 3455 recipes that made Waldorf great; cream of French, German, American cooking, in all categories. Full instructions, easy home use. 1896 edition. 907pp. 6⅝ x 9⅜.   20790-0 Clothbd. $15.00

COOKING WITH BEER, Carole Fahy. Beer has as superb an effect on food as wine, and at fraction of cost. Over 250 recipes for appetizers, soups, main dishes, desserts, breads, etc. Index. 144pp. 5⅜ x 8½. (Available in U.S. only)   23661-7 Pa. $2.50

STEWS AND RAGOUTS, Kay Shaw Nelson. This international cookbook offers wide range of 108 recipes perfect for everyday, special occasions, meals-in-themselves, main dishes. Economical, nutritious, easy-to-prepare: goulash, Irish stew, boeuf bourguignon, etc. Index. 134pp. 5⅜ x 8½.
23662-5 Pa. $2.50

DELICIOUS MAIN COURSE DISHES, Marian Tracy. Main courses are the most important part of any meal. These 200 nutritious, economical recipes from around the world make every meal a delight. "I . . . have found it so useful in my own household,"—N.Y. Times. Index. 219pp. 5⅜ x 8½.   23664-1 Pa. $3.00

FIVE ACRES AND INDEPENDENCE, Maurice G. Kains. Great back-to-the-land classic explains basics of self-sufficient farming: economics, plants, crops, animals, orchards, soils, land selection, host of other necessary things. Do not confuse with skimpy faddist literature; Kains was one of America's greatest agriculturalists. 95 illustrations. 397pp. 5⅜ x 8½.
20974-1 Pa.$3.95

A PRACTICAL GUIDE FOR THE BEGINNING FARMER, Herbert Jacobs. Basic, extremely useful first book for anyone thinking about moving to the country and starting a farm. Simpler than Kains, with greater emphasis on country living in general. 246pp. 5⅜ x 8½.
23675-7 Pa. $3.50

A GARDEN OF PLEASANT FLOWERS (PARADISI IN SOLE: PARADISUS TERRESTRIS), John Parkinson. Complete, unabridged reprint of first (1629) edition of earliest great English book on gardens and gardening. More than 1000 plants & flowers of Elizabethan, Jacobean garden fully described, most with woodcut illustrations. Botanically very reliable, a "speaking garden" of exceeding charm. 812 illustrations. 628pp. 8½ x 12¼.   23392-8 Clothbd. $25.00

ACKERMANN'S COSTUME PLATES, Rudolph Ackermann. Selection of 96 plates from the Repository of Arts, best published source of costume for English fashion during the early 19th century. 12 plates also in color. Captions, glossary and introduction by editor Stella Blum. Total of 120pp. 8⅜ x 11¼.   23690-0 Pa. $4.50

MUSHROOMS, EDIBLE AND OTHERWISE, Miron E. Hard. Profusely illustrated, very useful guide to over 500 species of mushrooms growing in the Midwest and East. Nomenclature updated to 1976. 505 illustrations. 628pp. 6½ x 9¼. 23309-X Pa. $7.95

AN ILLUSTRATED FLORA OF THE NORTHERN UNITED STATES AND CANADA, Nathaniel L. Britton, Addison Brown. Encyclopedic work covers 4666 species, ferns on up. Everything. Full botanical information, illustration for each. This earlier edition is preferred by many to more recent revisions. 1913 edition. Over 4000 illustrations, total of 2087pp. 6⅛ x 9¼. 22642-5, 22643-3, 22644-1 Pa., Three-vol. set $24.00

MANUAL OF THE GRASSES OF THE UNITED STATES, A. S. Hitchcock, U.S. Dept. of Agriculture. The basic study of American grasses, both indigenous and escapes, cultivated and wild. Over 1400 species. Full descriptions, information. Over 1100 maps, illustrations. Total of 1051pp. 5⅜ x 8½. 22717-0, 22718-9 Pa., Two-vol. set $12.00

THE CACTACEAE,, Nathaniel L. Britton, John N. Rose. Exhaustive, definitive. Every cactus in the world. Full botanical descriptions. Thorough statement of nomenclatures, habitat, detailed finding keys. The one book needed by every cactus enthusiast. Over 1275 illustrations. Total of 1080pp. 8 x 10¼. 21191-6, 21192-4 Clothbd., Two-vol. set $35.00

AMERICAN MEDICINAL PLANTS, Charles F. Millspaugh. Full descriptions, 180 plants covered: history; physical description; methods of preparation with all chemical constituents extracted; all claimed curative or adverse effects. 180 full-page plates. Classification table. 804pp. 6½ x 9¼. 23034-1 Pa. $10.00

A MODERN HERBAL, Margaret Grieve. Much the fullest, most exact, most useful compilation of herbal material. Gigantic alphabetical encyclopedia, from aconite to zedoary, gives botanical information, medical properties, folklore, economic uses, and much else. Indispensable to serious reader. 161 illustrations. 888pp. 6½ x 9¼. (Available in U.S. only) 22798-7, 22799-5 Pa., Two-vol. set $11.00

THE HERBAL or GENERAL HISTORY OF PLANTS, John Gerard. The 1633 edition revised and enlarged by Thomas Johnson. Containing almost 2850 plant descriptions and 2705 superb illustrations, Gerard's *Herbal* is a monumental work, the book all modern English herbals are derived from, the one herbal every serious enthusiast should have in its entirety. Original editions are worth perhaps $750. 1678pp. 8½ x 12¼. 23147-X Clothbd. $50.00

MANUAL OF THE TREES OF NORTH AMERICA, Charles S. Sargent. The basic survey of every native tree and tree-like shrub, 717 species in all. Extremely full descriptions, information on habitat, growth, locales, economics, etc. Necessary to every serious tree lover. Over 100 finding keys. 783 illustrations. Total of 986pp. 5⅜ x 8½. 20277-1, 20278-X Pa., Two-vol. set $10.00

AMERICAN BIRD ENGRAVINGS, Alexander Wilson et al. All 76 plates. from Wilson's *American Ornithology* (1808-14), most important ornithological work before Audubon, plus 27 plates from the supplement (1825-33) by Charles Bonaparte. Over 250 birds portrayed. 8 plates also reproduced in full color. 111pp. 9⅜ x 12½. 23195-X Pa. $6.00

CRUICKSHANK'S PHOTOGRAPHS OF BIRDS OF AMERICA, Allan D. Cruickshank. Great ornithologist, photographer presents 177 closeups, groupings, panoramas, flightings, etc., of about 150 different birds. Expanded *Wings in the Wilderness*. Introduction by Helen G. Cruickshank. 191pp. 8¼ x 11. 23497-5 Pa. $6.00

AMERICAN WILDLIFE AND PLANTS, A. C. Martin, et al. Describes food habits of more than 1000 species of mammals, birds, fish. Special treatment of important food plants. Over 300 illustrations. 500pp. 5⅜ x 8½. 20793-5 Pa. $4.95

THE PEOPLE CALLED SHAKERS, Edward D. Andrews. Lifetime of research, definitive study of Shakers: origins, beliefs, practices, dances, social organization, furniture and crafts, impact on 19th-century USA, present heritage. Indispensable to student of American history, collector. 33 illustrations. 351pp. 5⅜ x 8½. 21081-2 Pa. $4.00

OLD NEW YORK IN EARLY PHOTOGRAPHS, Mary Black. New York City as it was in 1853-1901, through 196 wonderful photographs from N.-Y. Historical Society. Great Blizzard, Lincoln's funeral procession, great buildings. 228pp. 9 x 12. 22907-6 Pa. $7.95

MR. LINCOLN'S CAMERA MAN: MATHEW BRADY, Roy Meredith. Over 300 Brady photos reproduced directly from original negatives, photos. Jackson, Webster, Grant, Lee, Carnegie, Barnum; Lincoln; Battle Smoke, Death of Rebel Sniper, Atlanta Just After Capture. Lively commentary. 368pp. 8⅜ x 11¼. 23021-X Pa. $8.95

TRAVELS OF WILLIAM BARTRAM, William Bartram. From 1773-8, Bartram explored Northern Florida, Georgia, Carolinas, and reported on wild life, plants, Indians, early settlers. Basic account for period, entertaining reading. Edited by Mark Van Doren. 13 illustrations. 141pp. 5⅜ x 8½. 20013-2 Pa. $4.50

THE GENTLEMAN AND CABINET MAKER'S DIRECTOR, Thomas Chippendale. Full reprint, 1762 style book, most influential of all time; chairs, tables, sofas, mirrors, cabinets, etc. 200 plates, plus 24 photographs of surviving pieces. 249pp. 9⅞ x 12¾. 21601-2 Pa. $6.50

AMERICAN CARRIAGES, SLEIGHS, SULKIES AND CARTS, edited by Don H. Berkebile. 168 Victorian illustrations from catalogues, trade journals, fully captioned. Useful for artists. Author is Assoc. Curator, Div. of Transportation of Smithsonian Institution. 168pp. 8½ x 9½. 23328-6 Pa. $5.00

THE SENSE OF BEAUTY, George Santayana. Masterfully written discussion of nature of beauty, materials of beauty, form, expression; art, literature, social sciences all involved. 168pp. 5⅜ x 8½.   20238-0 Pa. $2.50

ON THE IMPROVEMENT OF THE UNDERSTANDING, Benedict Spinoza. Also contains *Ethics, Correspondence,* all in excellent R. Elwes translation. Basic works on entry to philosophy, pantheism, exchange of ideas with great contemporaries. 402pp. 5⅜ x 8½.   20250-X Pa. $4.50

THE TRAGIC SENSE OF LIFE, Miguel de Unamuno. Acknowledged masterpiece of existential literature, one of most important books of 20th century. Introduction by Madariaga. 367pp. 5⅜ x 8½.
20257-7 Pa. $3.50

THE GUIDE FOR THE PERPLEXED, Moses Maimonides. Great classic of medieval Judaism attempts to reconcile revealed religion (Pentateuch, commentaries) with Aristotelian philosophy. Important historically, still relevant in problems. Unabridged Friedlander translation. Total of 473pp. 5⅜ x 8½.   20351-4 Pa. $5.00

THE I CHING (THE BOOK OF CHANGES), translated by James Legge. Complete translation of basic text plus appendices by Confucius, and Chinese commentary of most penetrating divination manual ever prepared. Indispensable to study of early Oriental civilizations, to modern inquiring reader. 448pp. 5⅜ x 8½.   21062-6 Pa. $4.00

THE EGYPTIAN BOOK OF THE DEAD, E. A. Wallis Budge. Complete reproduction of Ani's papyrus, finest ever found. Full hieroglyphic text, interlinear transliteration, word for word translation, smooth translation. Basic work, for Egyptology, for modern study of psychic matters. Total of 533pp. 6½ x 9¼. (Available in U.S. only)   21866-X Pa. $4.95

THE GODS OF THE EGYPTIANS, E. A. Wallis Budge. Never excelled for richness, fullness: all gods, goddesses, demons, mythical figures of Ancient Egypt; their legends, rites, incarnations, variations, powers, etc. Many hieroglyphic texts cited. Over 225 illustrations, plus 6 color plates. Total of 988pp. 6⅛ x 9¼. (Available in U.S. only)
22055-9, 22056-7 Pa., Two-vol. set $12.00

THE ENGLISH AND SCOTTISH POPULAR BALLADS, Francis J. Child. Monumental, still unsuperseded; all known variants of Child ballads, commentary on origins, literary references, Continental parallels, other features. Added: papers by G. L. Kittredge, W. M. Hart. Total of 2761pp. 6½ x 9¼.
21409-5, 21410-9, 21411-7, 21412-5, 21413-3 Pa., Five-vol. set $37.50

CORAL GARDENS AND THEIR MAGIC, Bronsilaw Malinowski. Classic study of the methods of tilling the soil and of agricultural rites in the Trobriand Islands of Melanesia. Author is one of the most important figures in the field of modern social anthropology. 143 illustrations. Indexes. Total of 911pp. of text. 5⅝ x 8¼. (Available in U.S. only)
23597-1 Pa. $12.95

THE PHILOSOPHY OF HISTORY, Georg W. Hegel. Great classic of Western thought develops concept that history is not chance but a rational process, the evolution of freedom. 457pp. 5⅜ x 8½.   20112-0 Pa. $4.50

LANGUAGE, TRUTH AND LOGIC, Alfred J. Ayer. Famous, clear introduction to Vienna, Cambridge schools of Logical Positivism. Role of philosophy, elimination of metaphysics, nature of analysis, etc. 160pp. 5⅜ x 8½. (Available in U.S. only)   20010-8 Pa. $1.75

A PREFACE TO LOGIC, Morris R. Cohen. Great City College teacher in renowned, easily followed exposition of formal logic, probability, values, logic and world order and similar topics; no previous background needed. 209pp. 5⅜ x 8½.   23517-3 Pa. $3.50

REASON AND NATURE, Morris R. Cohen. Brilliant analysis of reason and its multitudinous ramifications by charismatic teacher. Interdisciplinary, synthesizing work widely praised when it first appeared in 1931. Second (1953) edition. Indexes. 496pp. 5⅜ x 8½.   23633-1 Pa. $6.00

AN ESSAY CONCERNING HUMAN UNDERSTANDING, John Locke. The only complete edition of enormously important classic, with authoritative editorial material by A. C. Fraser. Total of 1176pp. 5⅜ x 8½.
20530-4, 20531-2 Pa., Two-vol. set $14.00

HANDBOOK OF MATHEMATICAL FUNCTIONS WITH FORMULAS, GRAPHS, AND MATHEMATICAL TABLES, edited by Milton Abramowitz and Irene A. Stegun. Vast compendium: 29 sets of tables, some to as high as 20 places. 1,046pp. 8 x 10½.   61272-4 Pa. $14.95

MATHEMATICS FOR THE PHYSICAL SCIENCES, Herbert S. Wilf. Highly acclaimed work offers clear presentations of vector spaces and matrices, orthogonal functions, roots of polynomial equations, conformal mapping, calculus of variations, etc. Knowledge of theory of functions of real and complex variables is assumed. Exercises and solutions. Index. 284pp. 5⅝ x 8¼.   63635-6 Pa. $4.50

THE PRINCIPLE OF RELATIVITY, Albert Einstein et al. Eleven most important original papers on special and general theories. Seven by Einstein, two by Lorentz, one each by Minkowski and Weyl. All translated, unabridged. 216pp. 5⅜ x 8½.   60081-5 Pa. $3.00

THERMODYNAMICS, Enrico Fermi. A classic of modern science. Clear, organized treatment of systems, first and second laws, entropy, thermodynamic potentials, gaseous reactions, dilute solutions, entropy constant. No math beyond calculus required. Problems. 160pp. 5⅜ x 8½.
60361-X Pa. $2.75

ELEMENTARY MECHANICS OF FLUIDS, Hunter Rouse. Classic undergraduate text widely considered to be far better than many later books. Ranges from fluid velocity and acceleration to role of compressibility in fluid motion. Numerous examples, questions, problems. 224 illustrations. 376pp. 5⅝ x 8¼.   63699-2 Pa. $5.00

AN AUTOBIOGRAPHY, Margaret Sanger. Exciting personal account of hard-fought battle for woman's right to birth control, against prejudice, church, law. Foremost feminist document. 504pp. 5⅜ x 8½.
20470-7 Pa. $5.50

MY BONDAGE AND MY FREEDOM, Frederick Douglass. Born as a slave, Douglass became outspoken force in antislavery movement. The best of Douglass's autobiographies. Graphic description of slave life. Introduction by P. Foner. 464pp. 5⅜ x 8½.   22457-0 Pa. $5.00

LIVING MY LIFE, Emma Goldman. Candid, no holds barred account by foremost American anarchist: her own life, anarchist movement, famous contemporaries, ideas and their impact. Struggles and confrontations in America, plus deportation to U.S.S.R. Shocking inside account of persecution of anarchists under Lenin. 13 plates. Total of 944pp. 5⅜ x 8½.
22543-7, 22544-5 Pa., Two-vol. set $9.00

LETTERS AND NOTES ON THE MANNERS, CUSTOMS AND CONDITIONS OF THE NORTH AMERICAN INDIANS, George Catlin. Classic account of life among Plains Indians: ceremonies, hunt, warfare, etc. Dover edition reproduces for first time all original paintings. 312 plates. 572pp. of text. 6⅛ x 9¼.   22118-0, 22119-9 Pa.. Two-vol. set $10.00

THE MAYA AND THEIR NEIGHBORS, edited by Clarence L. Hay, others. Synoptic view of Maya civilization in broadest sense, together with Northern, Southern neighbors. Integrates much background, valuable detail not elsewhere. Prepared by greatest scholars: Kroeber, Morley, Thompson, Spinden, Vaillant, many others. Sometimes called Tozzer Memorial Volume. 60 illustrations, linguistic map. 634pp. 5⅜ x 8½.
23510-6 Pa. $7.50

HANDBOOK OF THE INDIANS OF CALIFORNIA, A. L. Kroeber. Foremost American anthropologist offers complete ethnographic study of each group. Monumental classic. 459 illustrations, maps. 995pp. 5⅜ x 8½.
23368-5 Pa. $10.00

SHAKTI AND SHAKTA, Arthur Avalon. First book to give clear, cohesive analysis of Shakta doctrine, Shakta ritual and Kundalini Shakti (yoga). Important work by one of world's foremost students of Shaktic and Tantric thought. 732pp. 5⅜ x 8½. (Available in U.S. only)
23645-5 Pa. $7.95

AN INTRODUCTION TO THE STUDY OF THE MAYA HIEROGLYPHS, Syvanus Griswold Morley. Classic study by one of the truly great figures in hieroglyph research. Still the best introduction for the student for reading Maya hieroglyphs. New introduction by J. Eric S. Thompson. 117 illustrations. 284pp. 5⅜ x 8½.   23108-9 Pa. $4.00

A STUDY OF MAYA ART, Herbert J. Spinden. Landmark classic interprets Maya symbolism, estimates styles, covers ceramics, architecture, murals, stone carvings as artforms. Still a basic book in area. New introduction by J. Eric Thompson. Over 750 illustrations. 341pp. 8⅜ x 11¼.
21235-1 Pa. $6.95

THE STANDARD BOOK OF QUILT MAKING AND COLLECTING, Marguerite Ickis. Full information, full-sized patterns for making 46 traditional quilts, also 150 other patterns. Quilted cloths, lame, satin quilts, etc. 483 illustrations. 273pp. 6⅞ x 9⅝. 20582-7 Pa. $4.50

ENCYCLOPEDIA OF VICTORIAN NEEDLEWORK, S. Caulfield, Blanche Saward. Simply inexhaustible gigantic alphabetical coverage of every traditional needlecraft—stitches, materials, methods, tools, types of work; definitions, many projects to be made. 1200 illustrations; double-columned text. 697pp. 8⅛ x 11. 22800-2, 22801-0 Pa., Two-vol. set $12.00

MECHANICK EXERCISES ON THE WHOLE ART OF PRINTING, Joseph Moxon. First complete book (1683-4) ever written about typography, a compendium of everything known about printing at the latter part of 17th century. Reprint of 2nd (1962) Oxford Univ. Press edition. 74 illustrations. Total of 550pp. 6⅛ x 9¼. 23617-X Pa. $7.95

PAPERMAKING, Dard Hunter. Definitive book on the subject by the foremost authority in the field. Chapters dealing with every aspect of history of craft in every part of the world. Over 320 illustrations. 2nd, revised and enlarged (1947) edition. 672pp. 5⅜ x 8½. 23619-6 Pa. $7.95

THE ART DECO STYLE, edited by Theodore Menten. Furniture, jewelry, metalwork, ceramics, fabrics, lighting fixtures, interior decors, exteriors, graphics from pure French sources. Best sampling around. Over 400 photographs. 183pp. 8⅜ x 11¼. 22824-X Pa. $5.00